The Laughter of Love

A Study of Robert Burns

Raymond J.S. Grant

Detselig Enterprises Limited
Calgary, Alberta

© 1986 **Raymond J.S. Grant**
Professor of English
The University of Alberta

Canadian Cataloguing in Publication Data

Grant, Raymond J.S.
The laughter of love

Bibliography: p.
ISBN 0-920490-55-7 (pbk.)
0-920490-58-1 (bound)
1. Burns, Robert, 1759-1796 — Criticism
and interpretation. I. Title.
PR4338.G72 1986   821'.6   C85-091442-6

Detselig Enterprises Limited
P.O. Box G 399
Calgary, Alberta T3A 2G3

SAN 115-0324

ISBN 0-920490-55-7 (paperback)
Printed in Canada   0-920490-58-1 (hardbound)

To my good friend,
J. Hebden Willox

Preface

Writing in 1949, Hilton Brown prefaced his essay *There Was A Lad* with the following quotation from Augustine Birrell:

> The biography of a celebrated man usually reminds me of the outside of a coastguardsman's cottage — all tar and whitewash.

The present volume is the tar and whitewash which a later lover of Burns would like to add to the gallons that have already flowed so freely since the death of the bard.

The writer's modest aim is to discuss the common man's Rabbie Burns, and this book is a simple labour of love rather than a presumptuous attempt to rival the scholarship and eloquence of its noted predecessors. Aware of marking the footsteps of such skilled commentators as Crawford, Daiches, De Lancey Ferguson and Hecht, the writer freely and gratefully acknowledges all his borrowings, both conscious and unconscious. For all errors, banalities, clichés, oversimplifications and bad jokes the blame must be laid firmly at the door of the author alone, who writes in the hope that he has not given too grievous offence to the shade of Robert Burns.

Photographs in this book were taken by the author, Raymond J.S. Grant

Robert Burns — Portrait Biography
by Ted Tilby

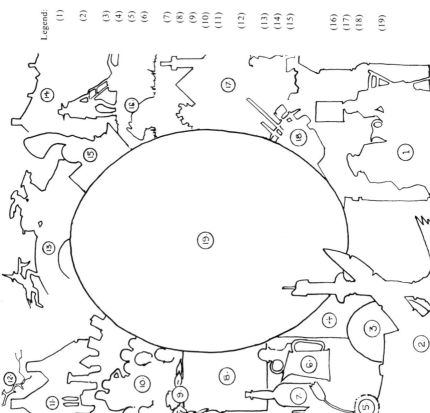

Legend:

(1) A friendly visit — in domestic setting typical of the area and times.

(2) Candlestick and writing paraphernalia to signify one of the most prolific and universally revered poets.

(3) Clarinda

(4) Burness-Campbell of Argyl (Original) Tartan

(5) 'To a Mountain Daisy'

(6) Inscription indicates Burn's membership in the Freemasons — went on to wear the apron of Deputy Master.

(7) Scotch drink ('Drink of the Free')

(8) The 'lovely Mrs. Norton'

(9) 'Oh my luve's like a red, red rose'

(10) The romantic life of Robert Burns.

(11) 'By some auld houlet-haunted biggin, or kirk deserted by her riggin' — Alloway Kirk.

(12) 'The speedy gleams the darkness swallow'd; loud, deep and lang the thunder bellow'd'

(13) 'A running stream they dar na cross' — Tam O'Shanter

(14) The birth place of Burns.

(15) The writer of such pieces as 'To a Mountain Daisy,' 'To a Mouse,' and 'On Seeing a Wounded Hare Limp By Me' — actually fired a pistol during the execution of his duties against the smugglers at Solway.

(16) 'To a Mouse'

(17) 'O, Let Me in This ae Night'

(18) 'The Cotter's Saturday Night' — hand tools used in his daily toil.

(19) "In his person he was tall and sinewy, and of such strength and activity, that Scott alone, of all the poets I have seen, seemed his equal: his forehead was broad, his hair black, with an inclination to curl, his visage uncommonly swarthy, his eyes large, dark and lustrous.'" — Allan Cunningham.

Contents

Ted Tilby is recognized as one of North America's foremost portrait artists and especially is noted for his portrait biographies.

Appreciation is expressed for permission to use "Robert Burns — Portrait Biography" for the cover of this book. A lithograph of this Portrait Biography is available.

Robert Burns Statue, Aberdeen

1
Sworn foe to sorrow, care, and prose, I rhyme away.

Let kings and courtiers rise and fa',
This world has mony turns,
But brightly beams abune them a'
The Star o' Rabbie Burns.

One beautiful April evening, the minister of a remote Highland parish called on one of the farmers in his congregation and found that worthy leaning on a gate and lost in contemplation of the lovely vista before him of heather-clad slopes and craggy peaks. Sharing the pleasant experience with the old man for several minutes, the minister was finally constrained to whisper softly, 'I to the hills will lift mine eyes.' 'Aye,' replied the old farmer, misty-eyed, 'Aye, Rabbie Burns was the boy!'

While this joke may be as old as the hills it mentions, like many a hoary and time-honoured witticism it enshrines a profound observation of some importance. On its own level, that of couthy, homespun, folk philosophy, the old farmer's response to the beauty before him is as significant as Faust's heart-felt cry, 'Verweile doch! Du bist so schön!' ('Stay now! Thou art so fair!'), on its more rarified level. The old farmer's instinctive rejoinder in its pithy brevity says more about the Robert Burns whose memory the whole world honours than volumes of learned literary criticism, but it also serves to encapsulate the problem which bedevils the writer in search of the essence of the poet's appeal. The joke is funny in Scotland, where the people grow up familiar with the metrical version of Psalm 121 appointed by the Church of Scotland to be used in worship and where the old farmer's automatic and incongruous confusion of David and Burns brings a ready laugh to the lips. A similarly endearing variant of the tale has the old farmer cry indignantly to a bemused English tourist, 'Ye've never heard o' Rabbie Burns? Awa', man, an' read yer Bible!' To seek to explain to the old farmer and to those in Scotland who share his sentiments what is meant by the title *The Laughter of Love* would be merely to preach to the converted.

Experience has shown that the joke falls rather flat outside Scotland or expatriate Scottish company and that attempts to explain why the story is funny are as doomed to failure as most efforts to analyse humour. Each nation has its particular and peculiar sense of what tickles the fancy, and ethnic humour is as a consequence very often simply untranslatable. In this instance, however, the effort is worth the making. The old farmer is not the sole beneficiary of the treasure of verse bequeathed by Robert Burns; he has to share the legacy with emigrants who have taken Burns's poetry to countless areas of the Old and the New World, with the descendants of those emigrants on all the earth's continents, and with those people throughout the world who are in no way racially, socially or historically related to the Scots but who yet venerate the poet's immortal memory. Burns's poetry appeals to the man in the street, be that street in Glasgow or Adelaide or Moscow or Rangoon or Tuktoyaktuk, and the old farmer, willy-nilly, must share the bounty with all other admirers of the poet. This is in a nutshell the enigma of Robert Burns, a writer at once so quintessentially Scottish that he is Scotland's national poet and at the same time so universal in his appeal that world-wide acclaim is given to his works and their sentiments. No other poet from any other country has this twin impact on his native heath and on the world as a whole, and the puzzle begs solution just as much as the joke craves explication. The old farmer must reveal his Rabbie Burns and share him with his brothers everywhere, with his fellow-beneficiaries of the poet's legacy of verse.

The present volume is an attempt to explain the joke and to solve the puzzle. It is hoped that from analysis of the institution of the Burns Supper, of the role of humour, of the image of the ploughman poet, of the biography, of the patriotic and political poetry, of the treatment of the Devil and Hell, of the handling of the topics of drink and the flesh, of the effects of satire, and of the pathos of the love poems there may emerge the essence of Burns and his poetry — the laughter of love.

'For me, an aim I never fash,' Burns tells us, 'I rhyme for fun . . . Sworn foe to sorrow, care, and prose, I rhyme away.' The laughter combats tears through love, and that love is expressed with sublime simplicity:

> Gie me ae spark o' Nature's fire,
> That's a' the learning I desire;
> Then tho' I drudge thro' dub an' mire
>   At pleugh or cart,
> My Muse, tho' hamely in attire,
>   May touch the heart.

This is the old farmer's Rabbie Burns, inspired by a Muse in homely garb who may nevertheless touch the heart, a poet whose warm creed can be so simply stated: 'but if I could, and I believe I do it as far as I can, I would wipe away all tears from all eyes.'

I am conscious that I see through a glass but darkly, and that I present perhaps only one facet of a multi-faceted and complicated poetic personality, but I shall count myself successful if one reader, one old farmer after perusing my work sets it down with the words, 'Aye, Rabbie Burns was the boy!'

Robert Burns Statue, Ayr

2

But now the Supper crowns their simple board

Fair fa' your honest, sonsie face,
Great Chieftain o' the Puddin-race!
Aboon them a' ye tak your place,
Painch, tripe, or thairm:
Weel are ye wordy of a grace
As lang's my arm.

Every January 25th, the *Address to the Haggis* heralds festivities all over the world in honour of the memory of Robert Burns. At the Burns Supper the food must include the traditional fare of haggis, neeps and tatties, and must be attended by suitable ceremonial — the saying of one of the Burns graces, the piping in of the haggis, the addressing and ritual cutting of the haggis, the toast to the Queen, the toast to the lassies, the lassies' reply, the toast to the Twa Lands of Scotland and Canada (or its equivalent in other countries boasting Scottish heritage), and the extended proposal of the toast to the Immortal Memory of the poet. The evening's entertainment may well include piping, Highland or Scottish Country dancing, recitation of Burns poems and the singing of Burns songs. All this is accompanied, of course, by generous draughts of Scotch whisky, without which a toast cannot be a toast at all or the Scottish poet's memory be suitably celebrated.

The central importance of the Burns Supper in the lives of Scots everywhere is well attested in the rubric to chapter 8 of *Punch on Scotland:*

The great westward movement of tribes across Europe over the years resulted in the Scots finding themselves trapped in a wet, misty cul-de-sac in the northern half of Britain with nowhere left to go except the Orkneys and Shetlands. As this seemed a poor solution, most of them have taken a deep breath and gone on to Canada, New Zealand, Australia, Samoa, the Far East and even, in desperate cases, London, where they have formed Caledonian societies and become even more fiercely Scottish than before. They turn out en masse twice a year, once

9

for Burns Night and once for Billy Connolly's world tour . . . .
For further details on that other great group of Scottish exiles,
Celtic and Rangers fans stranded abroad, see the chapter on
Sport.[1]

The institution of the Burns Supper is not always fully appreci-
ated by outsiders. One learns early to ignore the opinions of English
commentators who are unanimous in their impression that the Scots
annually stir up an alcoholic fog on January 25th to conceal the fact
that Caledonia has only one poet, and one of indifferent merit at that.
Such calumnies began with Matthew Arnold,[2] and persist, to no-one's
great surprise, south of the Border. But turning to Scottish writers
reveals there, too, less expected misunderstandings and some surprising detractors of Burns Night. Here, for instance, is Alistair Maclean
in *Introducing Scotland:*

> Wherever two or three Scots are gathered together, be it in Surrey
> or be it in Tierra del Fuego, they will immediately set about form-
> ing a St Andrew's Society and, inevitably, a Burns Society. The
> ostensible purpose of the former is to sustain and strengthen the
> cultural links with Scotia stern and wild by singing a very limited
> selection of purely Lowland songs — not Highland, for the odds
> are heavy that none of those present speaks Gaelic — filling a
> confined space with the hideous banshee wailing of the bagpipes,
> dancing the Highland fling in calf-length kilts and, in general,
> making themselves ridiculous. The Burns Societies' dinners, alleg-
> edly dedicated to the preservation and honouring of the memory
> of the immortal bard, should, on the face of it, be even more cul-
> tural occasions were it not for the fact that for the majority of
> people at the majority of such gatherings Burns is synonymous not
> with poetry but with haggis and an endless river of Scotch: it is
> compulsory, nay, it is a sacred duty, to drink to the poet's memory
> and hopeful health in the hereafter: no such ludicrous degree of
> obligation attaches to the actual reading of his poetry.[3]

Worse, the literary establishment joins in the censure of the Burns
Supper. For instance, Hugh MacDiarmid, himself writing in the tradition of Burns, talks disparagingly of the efforts of the Burns Night
orator in the following derogatory terms:

> . . . the witless lucubrations of the hordes of bourgeois 'orators'
> who annually befoul (Burns's) memory by the expression of sen-
> timents utterly antipathetic to that stupendous element in him

which ensured his fame . . (The Burns cult) knows nothing about
him or his work . . . except the stupid and stereotyped sentiments
it belches out annually.[4]

On this side of the Atlantic, a recent reviewer is gentler but no less
uncomplimentary when he writes:

> Burns has suffered terribly at the hands of the exponents of Scot-
> tish sentimentality and nostalgia. Fragments of his works are
> quoted out of context and the highly complex figure of Burns has
> been reduced to the, usually ex-patriate, Scot's fond image of him-
> self. In Canada he emerges as a cross between Harry Lauder and
> Andrew Carnegie, the shrewd, canny, worldly-wise but slightly
> ludicrous Scot.[5]

At least the reviewer, a Dr. Burns, disclaims any relationship. The
book under review, a selection of poems of Burns made by David
Daiches, contains in its introduction the apparently mandatory reference to 'all the flatulent nonsense talked at Burns Suppers.'[6]

This unthinking blanket condemnation of the Burns Supper from
the Olympian height of the ivory tower of academe would be more
damaging were it relevant. The toast to the Immortal Memory is *not*
an academic lecture, however — God forfend! — and in its different
format and context frequently results in addresses of high calibre, in
assessments of Burns of a high degree of excellence. It is the difficult
task of the Burns Night orator to explain the universal popularity of
the old farmer's Rabbie Burns and to propose a toast in honour of the
poet of the man in the street. This Rabbie Burns may not be the same
in all respects as the Robert Burns whose shade stalks the dusty cor-
ridors of academe; let academe, therefore, set aside disdain and take
note. For his part, the Burns Night orator will feel a justifiable pride
and satisfaction if his audience at the end of his toast join the old
farmer in saying, 'Aye, Rabbie Burns was the boy!'

One must put alongside the strictures of academe the *Epistle to
J. Lapraik* in which Burns at once defines his working poetic and
provides the most fitting retort to his scholarly detractors:

I am nae Poet, in a sense,
But just a Rhymer like by chance,
An' hae to Learning nae pretence,
              Yet, what the matter?
Whene'er my Muse does on me glance,
              I jingle at her.

Your Critic-folk may cock their nose,
And say, 'How can you e'er propose,
'You wha ken hardly verse frae prose,
              'To mak a sang?'
But, by your leaves, my learned foes,
              Ye're maybe wrang.

What's a' your jargon o' your Schools,
Your Latin names for horns an' stools;
If honest Nature made you fools,
              What sairs your Grammars?
Ye'd better taen up spades and shools,
              Or knappin-hammers.

A set o' dull, conceited Hashes,
Confuse their brains in Colledge-classes!
They gang in Stirks, and come out Asses,
              Plain truth to speak;
An' syne they think to climb Parnassus
              By dint o' Greek!

Gie me ae spark o' Nature's fire,
That's a' the learning I desire;
Then, tho' I drudge thro' dub an' mire
              At pleugh or cart,
My Muse, tho' hamely in attire,
              May touch the heart.

This is the old farmer's Rabbie Burns, the Rabbie Burns of whom the
Burns Night orator must speak in the hope that amidst his 'witless
lucubrations' and 'flatulent nonsense' may be caught a glimpse of the
poet which is invisible from the heights of Olympus.

Writing in the first century A.D., the Roman professor of rhetoric, Quintilian, gave a definition which has stood the test of almost two thousand years when he sought to describe the sort of orator appropriate for a Burns Supper:

> I am not unwilling that the man who has got to make a speech should show signs of nervousness when he rises to his feet, should change colour and make it clear that he feels the risks of his position: indeed, if these symptoms do not occur naturally, it will be necessary to simulate them. But the feeling that stirs us should be due to the realisation of the magnitude of our task and not to fear: we should be moved, but not to the extent of collapsing. But the best remedy for such excess of modesty is confidence: however great our natural timidity of mien, we shall find strength and support in the consciousness of the nobility of our task.[7]

Certainly the Burns Night orator can be no shrinking violet if he is to survive the risks of a position which requires him to face a large number of robust fellow-revellers; rather he must through his stentorian tones and flashing eye quell those mutinous members of his audience who seek to remind him from time to time either of Polonius' joke about brevity and the soul of wit or of W.H. Auden's remark that 'A professor is one who talks in someone else's sleep.' Disquieting, too, is this snippet of overheard conversation: 'What comes after his speech?' 'Wednesday!'

Even more daunting is Dr. Johnson's definition of a post-prandial speaker:

> He only has a right to suppose that he can express his thoughts with perspicacity or elegance, who has carefully perused the best authors, accurately noted their diversities of style, diligently selected the best modes of diction, and familiarised them by long habits of attentive practice.

No-one, perforce, would dare to claim to satisfy these lofty requirements save, of course, Dr. Johnson himself, the grand-master of the one-sided conversation. On one of the good doctor's points, however, Burns Night orators should stand firm — the appropriateness of one's diction. In proposing the toast to the Immortal Memory, many a speaker succumbs to the temptation to be grandiloquent, to use high-sounding words and high-flown rhetoric in praise of the man whose memory is being honoured. But when one remembers that it is Robert

Burns under discussion, it is obvious that such eulogy is quite out of place; Burns was not a god, he was not a hero, he was not a paragon of virtue — rather he was a hard-working Ayrshire farmer, a man of warmth and weaknesses, a man of humility and humanity, a complex human being, no more, if no less. Too often the toasts are a byword for rhetorical panegyric, solemn eulogy or mawkish sentimentality, all of which are tones unbefitting the spirit of Burns and threatening to justify at least in part some of the disdain of scholarship. Burns Night orators must not do Burns's memory a disservice by making him out to have been something he was not, as David Daiches points out:

> No lyric poet has been as much talked about and as often misunderstood as Robert Burns. In the conventional academic literary histories he is regarded as a 'pre-Romantic', the representative of a 'new spirit' which was to lead English poetry to greater glories in the nineteenth century; while in the annual Burns Night speeches of enthusiasts his significance as Scottish poet and literary craftsman is wholly obscured in mists of sentimental oratory. Burns was, in fact, neither a pre-Romantic nor the ideal Rotarian. . . .[8]

In appreciation of the Scottish bard, then, one must take the attitude Dr. Johnson took towards the English bard when he said of Shakespeare, 'I loved the man, and do honour his memory, on this side idolatry, as much as any.' 'On this side idolatry' — this warning should be placed on a card and nailed to the lectern of every proposer of the Immortal Memory.

I would, without apology, make the further demand of a Burns Night that where possible the speaker be a native Scot. If Burns be indeed Scotland's national poet, my chauvinistic demand is justified on two major counts: a native Scot can make the poetry sound as it should, and a native Scot knows enough about Scots humour not to go astray in interpretation of that poetry. It would be churlish to recount occasions on which non-Scots have been in action at Burns suppers with less than happy results, but I know I shall be forgiven for recounting briefly my first experience of hearing someone other than a native Scot read and discuss Burns. I frequently attend the meetings of an 18th-century scholarly society despite the best efforts of successive secretaries to omit my name from mailing-lists, and I much enjoy learned and convivial company under their auspices. One year an American scholar delivered a fine analysis of *The Jolly Beggars* which disconcerted me on precisely the counts I have mentioned;

the paper was serious throughout, and the quotations included in the presentation simply did not sound right to my ears. In addition to not being a Scot, the lecturer had the further disadvantage that his main scholarly interest lay in the works of Blake, whose 'Tiger, tiger, burning bright' has always made me wonder irreverently what sort of pyromaniac poet would set an animal on fire; certainly Blake's rather sombre Muse does not seem to me to have much in common with her merrier Caledonian counterparts. The end effect of the paper was to put before the society a Robert Burns somewhat different from the one I know and to lead me at a subsequent meeting to attempt a humorous corrective.

On the topic of the orator's nationality I should in Scotland itself be merely preaching to the converted; on certain more vexed questions concerning the details of the correct pronunciation of Burns's poetry I should not, however, find such unanimity of response. I do not think there really is one 'true Burns accent' in which to read his poetry today any more than there was one in the eighteenth century, for Burns wrote in a *variety* of accents and on a matching *variety* of levels of language, ranging from the homely vernacular of the unlettered rustic to the elegant literary English of the Augustan establishment. Two centuries of sound-change have now intervened to complicate matters further and to present to even a modern-day Ayrshire man reading the most local Burns poems vocabulary items and sounds no longer current and rhymes no longer true. Although Ayrshire provides some very eloquent and able advocates of Robert Burns (the Rev. James Currie and the Rev. John Weir Cook being fine examples), it does not follow necessarily that effective orators and singers of Burns's songs come only from the poet's own part of the world. After all, the poet's father, William Burness, was the son of a farmer in Kincardineshire,[9] and the poet's life was by no means restricted to Ayrshire and Dumfriesshire. Burns knew Edinburgh like the back of his hand, made several tours of the Highlands, toured the Borders and, as exciseman, haunted the Solway Firth. Robert Burns is not just local Ayrshire poet; he is *Scotland's national* poet, and it is valid for any Scot to attempt his public assessment and praise.

Similar objections from 'purists' attend the piping-in of the haggis and the habit of participants in Burns Suppers wearing Highland dress, the 'purists' feeling that Burns the Ayrshire Lowlander would disapprove of both as alien to his experience of Scotland. Again, justification lies in the fact that Burns is not restricted in his importance merely to Ayrshire. If his spirit flinches at the sight of my large frame clad in Ancient Grant kilt with all the trimmings, it would recoil with equal disgust from the English evening dress which would be even more alien to the 18th-century code of dress. John Cairney cannot attend every Burns Supper! One is reminded, however, of the little boy watching his father struggling into his kilt jacket on January 25th who asked, 'Daddy, why do you insist on wearing that jacket when you know very well you'll have an awful headache tomorrow morning?'

The Burns Supper has, of course, evolved over the years into something rather different from the first one. The first Burns Club was that founded in Greenock within just five years of the poet's death, and the first celebration of his birthday was held in Greenock in 1802. In the following year, the members hit on the idea of having the Burns Supper in Burns's cottage at Alloway on the anniversary of the poet's birth. This involved them in what was then an arduous midwinter coach trip from Greenock to Alloway on the evening of Friday, January 28th, 1803, and in a return journey the next evening. The members were under the mistaken impression given them by Currie's *Life and Works* that the poet was born on January 29th, 1759, not the 25th, and only later did scrutiny of the Ayr Parish Register reveal the error. Indeed, the second Burns Club to be formed, the Paisley Burns Club, held their celebrations on the 29th until 1818.[10] Since these early Burns Nights, the tradition has flourished of celebrating the poet's birth with a special ceremonial meal, and the institution of the Burns Supper has gone from strength to strength until now people of all races, all creeds and all countries celebrate the poet's birthday throughout the world every January 25th. In the bicentenary in 1959, it was estimated that 10,000 Burns Suppers were held in Scotland alone, but it is almost impossible to say just how many groups now get together once a year for the traditional meal of haggis, neeps and tatties complemented by generous helpings of usquebaugh and panegyric.

The menu of the Burns Supper has its detractors, a recent example being Richard Gordon. Talking of whisky in Scottish life, he recalls:

There was, for instance, the marvelous custom of washing the bride with it on her wedding night. When Shelley married Harriet Westbrook, their Edinburgh landlord knocked at the bedroom door with this in mind, but the poet tried to blow his head off. Whisky is also involved with Hogmanay, a festival defined by Evelyn Waugh as 'people being sick on the pavement in Glasgow.' And it is involved with Burns Night, when pipers herald the arrival in the banqueting room of the traditional haggis which is borne to the guest of honour and subsequently stabbed by him with his skean-dhu. But no Scotsman has ever tasted haggis; they are by then all so full of whisky that they could be eating the potting-compost boiled in an old sock which it so closely resembles.[11]

Well, really. The man is mistaken, of course — people certainly *do* taste the haggis; that is part of the problem eloquently stated by Patrick Ryan:

> The Scottish mind is inhabited by the Peculiar Haggis Hallucination which leads the sufferer to believe that this flaccid lump is his native ambrosia, whereas its recipe openly proclaims it to be a type of Boiled Butcher's Dustbin. The Scots make haggis from those intimate parts of animals which all other nations but the vultures throw away. Finding that they could sell all their guid meat at high profit to the English, they forced the remnant offal on their own stomachs, thus making a national delicacy out of an economic necessity. To perpetrate a haggis, you chop up a sheep's entrails with onion, suet and oatmeal, mix with nutmeg, lemon-juice and stock, cram the resulting sad splodge into the animal's paunch, stitch up and boil for three hours. The outcome is a sort of Offal Steamed Pudding, which looks like a pale castrated bag-pipe, tastes like savoury cardboard, and is monstrously productive of the wind.[12]

After Burns Suppers I am often approached by earnest enquirers. There are those who wish to know what the Devil I actually said to the haggis before slaughtering it, although the poem loses too much in translation for me to answer this satisfactorily, and there are those already feeling the first onslaughts of heartburn who are anxious to know what are the component parts of haggis. The latter question is of the same order as the enquiry as to what is worn beneath the kilt, and invites similarly facetious replies. I am sometimes tempted to refer the inquirers for information on this heavenly delicacy to the Old Testament, where between *Zephaniah* and *Zechariah* may be found the book of *Haggai*. In other words, I adopt the stance of the old Scot who told his English interlocutor, 'Sir, we boil it in a sheep's bag because such was the primitive way: it was invented, sir, before linen was thought of: and as for what it is made of, I dare not trust myself with telling — I can never name all the savoury items without tears.'

In his autobiography, John Galt records his taking a similar approach to an anxious Englishman. Galt recalls sitting opposite the Duke of York at a Burns Supper and being asked by his Royal Highness when the haggis was served, 'Galt, what is that?' Galt replied gravely, 'A boiled pair of bagpipes.' He then notes, 'His Royal Highness immediately ordered the "Great chieftain of the pudding race" ignominiously away.'[13]

The haggis is a dish peculiar to Scotland, though supposed to be of French origin ultimately and to be first cousin to the French 'hachis.' Haggis is a peasant dish, and like so many of the world's famous national dishes is designed as a beef substitute for those who cannot afford good meat, taking its place in this regard alongside curry, goulash, pasta, Irish stew, and the like. It is made of the minced offal of mutton, mixed with oat-meal and suet, and boiled in a sheep's stomach after being highly spiced and well seasoned. Here is a more detailed recipe from the *Edinburgh Evening News*:

> *Ingredients:* 1 sheep's stomach bag; 1 sheep's pluck (heart, liver and lights); 1/2 lb minced beef suet; 2 teacups toasted oatmeal; 4 onions, parboiled; 1 pint pluck boilings; pepper, salt and Jamaica pepper.
>
> *Method:* Wash bag well in cold water, then put into hot water and scrape thoroughly. Leave bag to soak in cold salted water overnight. Wash pluck and put into pan with the windpipe over the side. Cover with boiling water, add 1 teaspoon salt and boil for two hours. Remove from pan, cool, and cut away windpipe. Grate a quarter of the liver (leaving the rest for another meal) and mince heart and lights. Add suet, onions and oatmeal ready-toasted brown. Add seasonings and 1 pint of the liquor in which the pluck was boiled. Mix well. Half fill bag with mixture, sew up, and put in pan of boiling water. Prick bag occasionally with a needle to prevent it from bursting. Boil for three hours before serving. (The mixture may be cooked for three hours in a stewpan with extra liquor, if no sheep's bag available.)

The haggis was already something of a national Scottish dish before Burns wrote his *Address*, as is witnessed by Robert Fergusson's Flyting of that inveterate Scotophobe, Dr. Johnson. Every schoolboy knows of the irascible doctor's definition of oats in his *Dictionary of the English Language* of 1755: 'OATS — a grain which in England is generally given to horses, but in Scotland supports the people.' Lord Ellibank made the only possible reply: 'Very true, sir, but where in the

world will you find such horses, and such people?' Also mindful of
Johnson's remark about oats and incensed at the splendid banquet to
which the principal and professors of the University of St.
Andrews
treated 'the lying loun' on August 19, 1773, Fergusson suggested to
the regents an alternative 'list o' gudely hamel gear' as a bill of fare
for 'Samy':

> *Imprimis*, then, a haggis fat,
> Weel tottl'd in a seything pat,
> Wi' *spice* and *ingans* weel ca'd thro',
> Had help'd to gust the stirrah's mow,
> And plac'd itsel in truncher clean
> Before the gilpy's glowrin een.
>
> *Secundo*, then a gude sheep's head
> Whase hide was singit, never flead,
> And four black trotters cled wi' girsle,
> Bedown his throat had learn'd to hirsle.
> What think ye neist, o' gude fat brose
> To clag his ribs? a dainty dose!
> And white and bloody puddins routh,
> To gar the Doctor skirl, O Drouth!

Less well known is the story of Johnson's trip to the Western
Highlands with Boswell on which the great man was persuaded to try
haggis. The testy old scholar ate a heaping helping, and the serving
girl timidly asked him what he thought of it. Johnson growled out the
comment that haggis was perhaps fit for swine, to which the girl
replied, 'In that case, doctor, will you be after wanting a second helping?'

In *Life Among the Scots*, Alastair Borthwick sings the praises
of the Scottish high tea, remarking, 'It is Scotland's only original
contribution to cookery except the haggis, which few visitors try twice.'
One might respond that they don't need to try haggis more than once,
for the taste will stay with them for some time. And certainly doubts
arise in the reveller's head when he learns that the first time haggis
was imported into Vancouver by the firm of James Reid-Inglis it could
not enter Canada as meat or as a food-stuff and eventually cleared
customs as fertilizer.

Those who dislike the taste of haggis have open to them an
energetic reaction not considered by Dr. Johnson, the ancient sport of

haggis throwing. Raw haggis is compressed into culinary cannon-balls about 15 cm in diameter and weighing half a kilogram, then tossed in fierce competition. The last hurl-out for which I have figures was the McEwans Lager World Haggis Hurling Championship held in Scotland in September, 1980. Competitors from the U.K., Ireland, America, Canada and Australia were scheduled to do battle royal for the world championship titles and to attempt to break the current records of 156 ft. 8 in. for men and 87 ft. for women. The latest record of 49.5 metres was set by Scotsman Alan Pettigrew in 1981 and has not been surpassed at the time of writing. *De gustibus disputandum non est!*

The genesis of Burns's *Address to the Haggis* is uncertain. It is usually held that Burns was asked to say grace over a haggis at the home of a friend, and the applause he received encouraged him to turn his extempore prose grace into the poem always recited at Burns Suppers, with the final stanza reading as follows:

> Ye Pow'rs wha mak mankind your care,
> And dish them out their bill o' fare,
> Auld Scotland wants nae skinking ware
> That jaups in luggies;
> But, if ye wish her gratefu' pray'r,
> Gie her a Haggis!

Such is the reading of the Second, or Edinburgh Edition of the poet's works of 1787. The poem was first published, however, in the *Caledonian Mercury* for December 19th, 1786, and *The Scots Magazine* for January, 1787, and it is important to note that the periodicals carried a different final stanza in which Burns once and for all links haggis and whisky firmly in his readers' minds:

> Ye Powers wha gie us a' that's gude,
> Still bless auld Caledonia's brood
> Wi' great John Barleycorn's heart's blude
> In stowps or luggies;
> And on our board that king o' food,
> A glorious Haggice.

In his *Address to the Haggis*, therefore, Scotland's national poet has linked Scotland's national dish with Scotland's national drink, and the enjoying of both together on his birthday is sanctioned by his indisputable authority.

The same association of festive delights is made in the two short graces which go by the title *On A Sheep's Head*. At dinner one night in the Globe Tavern in Dumfries, Burns spoke the following extempore grace;

> O Lord, when hunger pinches sore,
> Do Thou stand us in stead,
> And send us from thy bounteous store
> A tup- or wether-head!
>   Amen.

After dinner, the poet continued in this vein:

> O Lord, since we have feasted thus,
> Which we so little merit,
> Let Meg now take away the flesh,
> And Jock bring in the spirit!
>   Amen.

While this cannot stand alongside the *Address to the Haggis* in poetic merit, it does serve to introduce the solution to a problem that can beset the Burns Supper, namely, when to say grace. Often the following grace is used, the one called *The Selkirk Grace* because it was the grace Burns spoke on a visit to St. Mary's Isle near Kircudbright and at the request of his host, the Earl of Selkirk:

> Some ha'e meat and canna eat,
> Some can eat that want it:
> But we ha'e meat and we can eat,
> Sae let the Lord be thankit.

The trouble with *The Selkirk Grace* is twofold; it can seem terribly hackneyed from its over-appearance and misquotation on wall-plaques, Irish linen tea-towels, picture-postcards and the like, and it is not always clear when it should be uttered — before the piper leads in the haggis, after the *Address to the Haggis*, or after the piper has departed and conversation has recommenced as the gourmets attack the delicacy before them. One effective answer to this quandary is to say an *after*-dinner grace when all have had their fill of haggis. My personal preference is for the simple but moving *Grace After Dinner:*

O Thou, in whom we live and move,
Who mad'st the sea and shore,
Thy goodness constantly we prove,
And grateful would adore.

And if it please thee, Pow'r above,
Still grant us with such store;
The Friend we trust; the Fair we love;
And we desire no more.

As the Burns Supper proceeds convivially, with the grace, the ceremonial dispatching of the haggis, the feasting, the toast to the monarch, the toast to the lassies, the lassies' response, the toast to the Twa Lands, the Immortal Memory, and the additional entertainment from pipers, singers, reciters and dancers, I am sure the spirit of Burns looks down benevolently, wishing well to those revelling in his honour. His blessing would no doubt take a form similar to that *To John Maxwell, of Terraughty, On His Birthday*, and would be heart-felt:

But for thy friends, and they are mony,
Baith honest men and lasses bony,
May couthie fortune, kind and cany,
        In social glee,
Wi' mornings blythe and e'enings funny
        Bless them and thee!

3
For brave Caledonia immortal must be

Thee, Caledonia, thy wild heaths among,
Famed for the martial deed, the heaven-taught song,
To thee, I turn with swimming eyes.

If the happy survivors of earlier Burns Suppers who have attended the slaughter of previous generations of haggis, who have participated with enthusiasm in toasts to the Immortal Memory, and who have learned to endure with a measure of equanimity that peculiar combination of headache, heartburn and hangover associated with the morning after were to ask themselves to analyse their motives for coming out annually to Burns Suppers, they might get some surprises. I did, a couple of years ago. One of my colleagues mentioned hearing one of my radio broadcasts one January evening. 'Was I talking about Burns?' I asked. 'Well,' he replied, 'You were *speaking* about Burns, but you were really *saying*, "I was born a Scotsman, I'll always be a Scotsman, I'll live and die a Scotsman."'

This shook me rather, until I realised that he was quite right. At this time of year Scots take their kilts out of mothballs, comb their sporrans, polish their skean-dubhs, put make-up on their knees and roughen their accents to get together in order to tell the world, and one another, how Scottish they are. For one night in the year at least, they are all Rob Roys of one kind or another, and damned proud of the fact. This is proven by the people who sidle up to me after the Immortal Memory to declare their lineage; someone named Todosichuk or Tishkowski will assure me, 'My great-grandmother was a MacGreagor,' or an African will say, 'There's Scottish blood in my veins, too — my great-grandfather was at the eating of a Scottish missionary!'

And out come the kilts, not only the traditional tartans which frightened the Romans of old, but all sorts of new-fangled ones; last century gave us the Victoria tartan and the Balmoral tartan, and now there's a Burns tartan, a fauchy-looking black dambrod which, thankfully, I've seen only in a jacket and not in the full horror of a kilt. Locally, the Alberta tartan takes third place to the vivid hues of the ancient Poderski and multi-coloured splendour of the hunting Rabinovitch. Old ancestral kilts are the best, of course, kilts that have seen action and weathered many a storm. And they must be of the right length; one recalls the remark made in 1822 to the noble lady who was concerned about the brevity of George IV's kilt: 'Never mind, His Majesty's visit is short too, so the more we see of him the better.'

Throughout history, Scotland's vexed relations with the Sassenachs have led to their making verbal as well as military attacks upon Caledonia, and these, too, must be repulsed. Think, for instance, of Shakespeare including in *The Merchant of Venice* the quite gratuitous remark, '. . . Others, when the bag-pipe sings i' the nose, Cannot contain their urine.' Shakespeare, of course, cannot be forgiven for *Macbeth* or for his not being entirely Scottish in descent which, as one critic remarked, 'is a great peety, for unquestionably the man had the abeelity tae maintain oor reputation.' The kindest epitaph Scots can accord the English bard is that given Lord Rosebery by T.W.H. Crosland in *The Unspeakable Scot* — 'sometimes he does brilliant things, but he cannot keep them up. In brief he is half Scotch and half soda.'

Or think of the many adverse comments made by Burns's English contemporary, Dr. Johnson, to the effect that 'Much may be made of a Scotchman, if he be caught young,' or, 'The noblest prospect which a Scotchman ever sees, is the high road that leads him to England.' Consider, too, the following Johnsonian calumny:

DR. JOHNSON: 'Sir, it is a very vile country.'
MR. S———:   'Well, Sir, God made it.'
DR. JOHNSON: 'Certainly he did, but we must remember that He made it for Scotchmen; and comparisons are odious, Mr. S———, but God made Hell.'

Charles Lamb complains in the *Essays of Elia*:

In my early life I had a passionate fondness for the poetry of Burns. I have sometimes foolishly hoped to ingratiate myself with his countrymen by expressing it. But I have always found that a true Scot resents your admiration of his compatriot, even more than he would your contempt of him.

Of course, no Englishmen 'claimin' ken' by quoting chunks of Burns to Scotsmen have anything to recommend them, so part of the Burns Night ritual is the telling of anti-English jokes.

While Scots sympathize with the 99% of the human race who are not fortunate enough to be of Scottish extraction, they reserve a particular brand of sentiment for the poor souls living to the south of the world's most important border. If has often been said, 'You can always tell an Englishman — but you cannot tell him much.' Yet some would say this is not true; it is not always possible to tell the Sassenachs apart — they all look alike. This, at any rate, was the experience of one Scottish businessman who went for a tour of England to further the interests of international trade. On his return to Scotland, he was asked how he found the Sassenachs. 'Och, I niver got tae ken ony o' them. I dealt only wi' the heids o' departments, and they were a' Scots. Fur instance, when I gaed tae the famous firm o' Winterbottom and Winterbottom, I askit fur ane o' the senior pairtners. "Which Mr. Winterbottom would you like to speak to, sir?" I was asked, "Mr. MacGreagor or Mr. McTavish?"'

The English, of course, do not talk English very well, and this can cause problems. A lady from Scotland set off for a vacation in England, and was asked upon her return to God's own country how she had communicated with the English. She replied, 'Och, it wiz easy — I jist drappit a' the R's an' gaed the words a bit chow i' the middle.'

Salutary indeed is the tale about the English lady resident in Edinburgh who was determined that everything she bought in Scotland should be of English origin. Matters came to a head one day when she told the butcher, 'I want a sheep's head, and be sure it's an English sheep's head.' The butcher promptly called to his assistant, 'Hey, Jock, bring ben a sheep's heid, bit first tak oot the brains!'

An Englishman who was a keen fisherman went on a fishing holiday to Scotland. Returning to his lodgings at the end of the first day without a fish to his name, he was amused to see a little Scots boy fishing with a length of old rope and a potato. 'I say,' the Englishman exclaimed, 'You'll never catch anything with that.' 'I'm no sae sure,' replied the wee boy, 'You're the fourth since dinner-time.' The same benighted Sassenach caught nothing all week, and was dismayed that at every meal his landlady fed him the finest of fish. He sent home to the south for a packet of sausages to introduce some variety into his diet, and gave them triumphantly to the landlady. Imagine his consternation when he came down to the dining-room and found on his plate only a heap of sausage skins. 'Ah weel,' explained his landlady, 'That's a' that wiz left o' yer English fish efter I'd guttid them!'

The best anti-English joke of all, the one I feel Burns would have approved the most, concerns the Englishman who took his wife to the Braemar Gathering for some real culture. It came on sleet as usual, and the wife demanded that her husband locate a raincoat for her. On his search, the Englishman burst into a tent containing some of the local athletes and exclaimed, 'I say, you chaps, I'm looking for a macintosh to cover my wife.' 'Och,' came the reply, 'I'm afraid we're a' MacGreagors here — wid ane o' us nae dae equally weel for the job?'

So at Burns Suppers the cause of Scottish patriotism is well served by the tradition of telling stories about the Scots' less fortunate neighbours born south of the Tweed, those puir gabblin' craiturs, the English. But the Scots must also tell jokes about *themselves*, for that is where a true sense of humour must start; just as, for instance, the Poles tell the best Polish jokes, the Ukrainians the best Ukrainian jokes and the Jews the best Jewish jokes, so the Scots tell the best Scottish jokes. They laugh, for example, at the Scotsman who won the Western Canadian Lottery and yet looked decidedly gloomy. 'It's this ither ticket, ye ken — I canna imagine why I bocht it.'

They smile at Nicholas Fairbairn's story of the old Islander explaining why he always followed his nip of whisky with a beer chaser: 'If ye just drink whisky ye get tight before ye're fu' and if ye just drink beer ye get fu' before ye're tight but if ye drink them together ye get fu' and tight at the same time and ye know when to stop.'[14]

A Scottish family were walking home from church in Aberdeen. 'Fit a puir sermon,' said the father. 'Fit dreadfu' singin,' said the mother. 'Fu badly the choir performed,' said the daughter. 'The prayers bored me stiff,' said the eldest son. After a few minutes of silence, the youngest child spoke. 'I thocht it wiz quite a guid show fur a penny!'

And how Burns would have enjoyed Forbes Macgregor's comparison of the poet and the villain Burke:

> When the phrenologists were in full swing about a century and a half ago they had the human head portioned off into allotments for twenty or more different faculties such as amativeness, aggressiveness, philoprogenitiveness and such 'lang-nebbit' words. Poor Burns's skull was exhumed in 1834 and awarded marks out of twenty for each of these characteristics. Surprisingly he did not

gain full marks for amativeness, though he did quite well for poetic ability. Burke, the multi-murderer, appears, in the main, to have had almost as good a score as Burns. Apart from the trifling matter of a few suffocations, we might have had Burke Suppers and Immoral Memories.[15]

Jokes at a Burns Supper are along the lines of the BBC's introduction to the pianist Semprini's radio programme — 'old ones, new ones, loved one, forgotten ones.' Yet two religious jokes involving Burns ought to be placed on record. 'Man, Jock,' said his friend, 'I never kent ye wiz a Catholic.' 'Ah'm nae a Catholic,' cried Jock, 'It's the Church o' Scotland I stay awa frae. What mad ye think I wiz a Catholic?' 'Weel, it's that picter o' the Pope hingin' on yer wall.' 'The Pope?' exclaimed Jock, 'I wish I could hae five meenits wi' the Aiberdonian that selt me the picter. He telt me it wiz a picter o' Rabbie Burns in his Freemason's apron!'

The biographies should be rewritten to include the irreverent tale of Burns's only visit to a Roman Catholic church. Touring far from home with a friend and arriving in a district strange to them both, Burns astonished his friend by going to confession. 'Forgive me, father, for I have sinned,' he confessed, 'I hae committed Adam's sin o' the flesh.' 'With whom did ye dae this?' asked the priest. 'Oh, faither, I canna tell ye the girlie's name.' 'Well, was it Mary McEwen? Maggie MacLeod? Peggy Maclaren?' 'I'm sorry, faither, but it wadnae be richt tae tell ye the quine's name.' 'Oh, well,' sighed the priest, 'Say ten *Aves* and ten *Paters* every night for a week.' When Burns came out of the church, his friend asked, 'Did that dae ony guid for yer soul?' And Burns replied, 'Na, na, but I got us the names o' three certainties!'

'Here's tae us! Wha's like us? Damn few, and they're a' deid!' This grand auld Scottish toast is used at many a Burns Supper to bid the guests welcome to the evening's celebration of the memory of Scotland's national poet and the world's only truly international poet. And the toast may legitimately be used anywhere in the world where Scots foregather in the name of Robert Burns. The bounds of Scottish patriotism extend to include the many parts of the world to which Scots have emigrated, either perforce or by choice, and Auld Scotia broadens her boundaries to enfold a Nova Scotia; Edinburgh salutes her younger sister Dunedin; Aberdeen greets other Aberdeens in Hong Kong, Dakota, Washington State; Perth hails a younger namesake in Australia. In North America, it is gratuitous really to point out the importance of Scotsmen in the foundation of the United States; Scotland has provided no fewer than fifteen presidents, while five Scots pipers buried their instruments before following Custer to Little Big Horn and two Scots died heroic deaths at the Alamo — Jim Bowie and Davie Crockett. Statues of Burns grace many a U.S. city, a fine example being the one looking over the Burns Triangle on the east side of Milwaukee presented to the city in 1909 by an emigré Scot by the name of James Bryden. There is even a replica of the Alloway cottage in Atlanta, Georgia.

Scotland's most distant colony is the Moon, for Neil Armstrong's name betrays his ethnic origin unerringly. Until the eventual establishment of a Lunar Colony, there is still plenty of opportunity for Burns Suppers on an Earth boasting over fifty million persons of Scots lineage. In Canada, it is customary at a Burns Supper to raise the glasses in a toast to the Twa Lands of Scotland and Canada. Relations between the two countries have always been close, and it is unnecessary to rehearse the long list of names of prominent Scots responsible for the formation of Canada, from the eastern seaboard to Vancouver, where the statue of Burns (an exact copy of that in Ayr) smiles benevolently over the city from its place of pride in Stanley Park. Suffice it to say that if God made Scotland, Scotsmen made Canada.[16]

Wherever men foregather in a spirit of good fellowship and enjoyment of good food, better whisky and the company of the ladies Burns would feel right at home, and at Canadian Burns Suppers he would enjoy being present to share Canadian jokes as well as Scottish ones. No-one would revel more than Burns in the story of the maiden speech in Ottawa of a certain Liberal member of parliament who must remain nameless. 'Pierre,' said a member of the Opposition, 'that was a Rolls Royce oration.' 'Qu' est-ce que c'est que vous dites là, "a Rolls Royce oration?"' 'Well,' said the Conservative, 'You were well oiled, barely audible, and seemed to run on for ever.'

The Canadians dwell enviously on stories of the poet's sexual prowess in their story of Burns's conversation with a girl at a party. 'May I take you home this evening?' he asked a beautiful blonde, 'I like taking experienced girls home.' 'I'm not an experienced girl,' demurred the blonde. 'You're nae home yet either,' replied Burns.

And he would equally enjoy the story of the Canadian who overindulged on January 25th and had to go to the doctor. 'Doctor,' he complained, 'ever since that Burns Supper, when I fall asleep at night

I see striped haggis.' 'Have you seen a psychiatrist?' asked the doctor. 'No, doctor, just striped haggis.'

Burns would delight in the famous remark by J.R. Colombo in 1965 to the effect that Canada could have enjoyed English government, French culture, and American know-how; instead it ended up with English know-how, French government, and American culture. Burns would surely sympathise with Mr. Trudeau's accountant who told his fellow-worker, 'For a minute this deficit really had me worried; I forgot I was working for the government.' Most of all, I think he'd treasure the story of the Inuit lady who was furious with her husband. 'Would you believe it?' she asked her friend, 'Last night he stayed out until half-past January!'

'Here's tae us! Wha's like us? Damn few, and they're a' deid!' Proposing this time-honoured and familiar toast has therefore the further purpose of setting the tone for the evening's festivities — good fellowship, a richt guid-willie waught for Auld Lang Syne, expression of noble Scottish sentiment, and a toast to the Immortal Memory of perhaps the greatest Scotsman of all. It sets the tone I consider to be appropriate for a Burns Night eulogy — partly light-hearted, partly deadly serious, assessment and adulation this side idolatry. The joke telling is very necessary. Aldous Huxley describes the vital role played in common humanity by spontaneous laughter:

> A little ruthless laughter clears the air as nothing else can do; it is good for us, every now and then, to see our ideals laughed at, our conception of nobility caricatured; it is good for solemnity's nose to be tweaked, for human pomposity to be made to look ridiculous.

This may be the aspect of Burns Suppers least well understood by scholars but contributing much to the popular benefit derived from the night's fellowship. Scots are not all Rob Roys, they don't all wear the kilt every day, they don't all have red hair or heather growing out the back of their necks, but once a year they get together to tell a few jokes about themselves and others that assert to the world their pride in being essentially Scottish. Alba Gu Brath!

To approve and indeed emphasize the levity and the laughter is *ipso facto* to take issue with those who deprecate the institution of Burns Night. The Burns Supper is a non-scholarly, or perhaps a *supra*-scholarly occasion, since through the laughter and its patriotism it is clear that Burns Night has obviously come over the years to mean much more to many more people than merely the reading and analysis of some of the better-known poems. Part of the purpose of attending Burns Night year after year is, through laughter and good fellowship, to assert eternal Scottishness and justify the ways of Burns to man. That there is also something *universally* attractive about this process serves to underline the complexity of the poet's appeal and its essential mystery.

At least part of the answer to the riddle of Burns's universal appeal must be that an echoing laughter is found in his works. Burns would enjoy being present to share the jokes and would, no doubt, tell some much more shocking than mine that would make one's hair stand on end. We can be sure of this because laughter is an all-pervading element of Burns's better poetry; without the laughter, one should have a grim Muse with which to deal and Burns would not be Burns. Consider his avowed purpose in writing poetry as he expresses it in his *Epistle to James Smith*, a Mauchline merchant and early friend:

> Just now I've taen the fit o' rhyme
> My barmie noddle's working prime,
> My fancy yerket up sublime
>   Wi' hasty summon:
> Hae ye a leisure-moment's time
>   To hear what's comin?
>
> Some rhyme a neebor's name to lash;
> Some rhyme, (vain thought!) for needfu' cash;
> Some rhyme to court the countra clash,
>   An' raise a din;
> For me, an aim I never fash;
>   I rhyme for fun.
>
> The star that rules my luckless lot,
> Has fated me the russet coat,
> An' damn'd my fortune to the groat;
>   But, in requit,
> Has blest me with a random-shot
>   O' countra wit.

And later in the same poem he asserts unequivocally:

> An anxious e'e I never throws
> Behint my lug, or by my nose;
> I jouk beneath Misfortune's blows
> As weel's I may;
> Sworn foe to sorrow, care, and prose,
> I rhyme away.

Here is a vital ingredient of Burns's practical poetic and philosophy — take serious things frivolously and frivolous things frivolously; laugh at life, laugh at the world, laugh at oneself; 'I rhyme for fun.' That the Muses of Caledonia are, indeed, intended to be nothing if not Merry can be seen, for instance, in the figures of pure humour that enliven *Tam o' Shanter*. Here is the nagging wife:

> Gathering her brows like gathering storm,
> Nursing her wrath to keep it warm. . . .
> She tauld thee weel thou was a skellum,
> A blethering, blustering, drunken blellum;
> That frae November till October,
> Ae market-day thou was nae sober;
> That ilka melder, wi' the miller,
> Thou sat as lang as thou had siller;
> That every naig was ca'd a shoe on,
> The smith and thee gat roaring fou on;
> That at the Lord's house, even on Sunday,
> Thou drank wi' Kirkton Jean till Monday.
> She prophesied that late or soon,
> Thou would be found deep drown'd in Doon;
> Or catch'd wi' warlocks in the mirk,
> By Alloway's auld haunted kirk.

This is the archetypal nagger at work, and how true to life ring her scolding tones!

A sense of humour is a faculty of the human mind without which no view of life can be comprehensive and true, and this Burns had in abundance. Try talking about Burns to a man without a sense of humour; it's like trying to describe the hues of the rainbow to one who is colour-blind. This is precisely where the older generation of Victorian critics of Burns went agley in taking the biography too literally and too seriously. Here, for instance, is T.W.H. Crosland in *The Unspeakable Scot*:

The real reason . . . why Burns became, and continues to be, a
sort of patron saint to the peoples North of the Tweed is . . . that
he was a libidinous writer, and a condoner of popular vices. Turn
where you will in his precious works, you will find that drunken-
ness and impropriety are matters for which he has unqualified
sympathy. Whiskey and women are the subjects which furnish
forth the majority of his flights . . . It is safe to say that a more
profligate person has never figured on the slopes of Parnassus.

People without a sense of humour will never understand Burns, for if
Burns's Caledonian Muses may be more economical than their English counterparts, they are primarily fun-loving. Some of Burns's lesser-
known, impromptu verses show his humour as well as his more famous
poems, and in shorter compass. Take, for instance, the occasion on
which he was trapped at a party at Terraughty in the company of a
braggart *nouveau-riche*; Burns's impromptu response silenced the
effete snob most effectively:

The Toadeater

No more of your titled acquaintances boast,
    Nor of the gay groups you have seen;
A crab louse is but a crab louse at last,
    Tho' stack to the (curl) of a Queen.

This is Burns the gentle satirist who seeks to emend behaviour by
laughter. This is Burns of *Holy Willie's Prayer* or of *To A Louse*, in
which Burns chides a lady who has gone to church to show off her
proud, new bonnet instead of to pray; a louse, unbeknown to the lady,
crawls up the back of her bonnet, and spoils the effect. Burns takes
the lady to task so gently in these famous lines:

Oh Jenny dinna toss your head,
An' set your beauties a' abread!
Ye little ken what cursed speed
            The blastie's makin!
Thae winks and finger-ends, I dread,
            Are notice takin!

Oh wad some Pow'r the giftie gie us
To see oursels as others see us!

> It wad frae monie a blunder free us
> An' foolish notion:
> What airs in dress an' gait wad lea'e us,
> An ev'n Devotion!

Robert Burns was no saint, and his was never the first name to come to mind when the minister was indisposed. Seldom was Burns a hypocrite, preferring the cathedral of nature in the great outdoors of farm life and normally not darkening the doors of the church. One Sunday, however, he was trapped by a winter storm at Lamington, in Clydesdale, and for want of diversion went to a church which he found too cold in too many ways. He left this impromptu epigram in his pew:

> As cauld a wind as ever blew;
> A caulder kirk, and in 't but few;
> As cauld a minister's ever spak;
> Ye'se a' be het or I come back.

This is the Burns of *The Holy Fair*, with its rival ministers preaching at one another and with the outcome of the festivities other than the ministers intend:

> How monie hearts this day converts,
> O' Sinners and o' Lasses!
> Their hearts o' stane, gin night are gane
> As saft as ony flesh is.
> There's some are fou o' love divine;
> There's some are fou o' brandy;
> An' monie jobs that day begin,
> May end in Houghmagandie
> Some ither day.

The humour can be ever so gentle, as in the impromptu stanza composed in the kirk in Duns, *To Miss Ainslie, In Church*, in which the poet tells Rachel Ainslie:

> Fair Maid, you need not take the hint,
> Nor idle texts pursue;
> 'Twas only sinners that he meant,
> Not angels such as you.

A similar smile plays on his lips in *The Book-Worms*. Finding on the table of a grand library an uncut, handsomely-bound but worm-eaten copy of the works of Shakespeare, Burns takes a sly dig at the English bard:

> Through and through the inspired leaves,
> Ye maggots, make your windings;
> But, oh! respect his lordship's taste,
> And spare his golden bindings.

This is the perfect corollary to the Exeter Book's *Riddle XLVII*, 'Moððe word fr æt' — 'A Moth Ate Words':

> A moth ate words. That seemed to me
> a strange event, when I heard of that wonder,
> that the worm, a thief in the darkness,
> should devour the song of a man, a famed utterance
> and a thing founded by a strong man. The thievish
>   visitant
> was no whit the wiser for swallowing the words.[17]

Fine examples of Burns's humour may be found in his epitaphs, such as that *On A Noisy Polemic*, James Humphrey, in life a mason, in death immortal as the famous 'Bleth'ran Bitch':

> Below thir stanes lie Jamie's banes;
> O Death, it's my opinion,
> Thou ne'er took such a bleth'ran bitch
> Into thy dark dominion!

Then there is the *Epitaph On A Henpecked Country Squire*:

> As father Adam first was fool'd,
> A case that's still too common,
> Here lyes a man a woman rul'd,
> The Devil rul'd the woman.

And the dominie of the parish school of Cleish, in Fife, enjoys a similar fame posthumously in *On A Schoolmaster*:

Here lie Willie Michie's banes,
O Satan, when ye tak him,
Gie him the schulin' o' your weans;
For clever Deils he'll mak 'em!

The *Epitaph on William Graham Esq. of Mossknow* has its sting in the tail:

'Stop thief!' dame Nature called to Death,
As Willie drew his latest breath:
'How shall I make a fool again —
My choicest model thou hast ta'en.'

On A Suicide brings Burns's humour at its most scathing, for Burns the lover of life and laughter can have no sympathy with the despairing cowardice of self-destruction:

Here lies in earth a root of Hell,
Set by the Deil's ain dibble;
This worthless body damned himsel,
To save the Lord the trouble.

Burns actually knew the Devil better than he did the Lord, as is shown in another of his impromptu verses. He found a painter in Edinburgh working on a picture of Jacob's dream and on the back of a sketch wrote the artist this instant criticism:

Dear ——, I'll gie ye some advice,
You'll tak it no uncivil:
You shouldna paint at angels, man,
But try and paint the Devil.

To paint an angel's kittle wark,
Wi' Nick there's little danger;
You'll easy draw a lang-kent face,
But no sae weel a stranger.

This is the Burns of the *Address to the Deil* and *The Deil's Awa wi' th' Exciseman,* but in more concentrated form.

Such examples of Burns's laughter could be multiplied, but I think sufficient have been adduced to demonstrate that laughter constitutes an important part of Burns's poetic. His Muse, he remarks in his *Second Epistle to Lapraik*, works 'off-the-cuff', for her inspirations are unpremeditated, spontaneous, extemporaneous:

> Sae I've begun to scrawl, but whether
> In rhyme, or prose, or baith thegither,
> Or some hotch-potch that's rightly neither,
>   Let time mak proof;
> But I shall scribble down some blether
>   Just clean aff-loof.

This is no serious Muse that intends to soar above the Aonian Mount. It is rather a down-to-earth Muse that laughs at herself first: 'scribble down some blether just clean aff-loof.'

The preface to the Kilmarnock Edition of July, 1786, contains Burns's avowal of his purpose in poetic composition:

> To amuse himself with the little creations of his own fancy, amid the toil and fatigues of a laborious life; to transcribe the various feelings, the loves, the griefs, the hopes, the fears, in his own breast; to find some kind of counterpoise to the struggles of a world, always an alien scene, a task uncouth to the poetical mind — these were his motives for courting the Muses, and in these he found poetry to be its own reward.

The jokes, the fellowship, the laugher at a Burns Supper therefore satisfy the desire annually to fling one's Scottish pride in the teeth of the world and to challenge other nations to match the Scots in honest self-appraisal through humour, but they achieve much more than this in that they set the stage appropriately for the Immortal Memory. The laughter paves the way for the love. 'I rhyme for fun,' says Burns; 'My Muse, tho' hamely in attire, may touch the heart.'

Robert Burns Statue, Vancouver

Detail from Burns Statue, Vancouver

4

I was bred to the plough, and am independent

> The simple Bard, rough at the rustic plough,
> Learning his tuneful trade from ev'ry bough;
> The chanting linnet, or the mellow thrush,
> Hailing the setting sun, sweet, in the green
>   thorn bush,
> The soaring lark, the perching red-breast shrill,
> Or deep-ton'd plovers, grey, wild-whistling o'er
>   the hill;
> Shall he, nurst in the Peasant's lowly shed,
> To hardy Independence bravely bred,
> By early Poverty to hardship steel'd,
> And train'd to arms in stern Misfortune's field,
> Shall he be guilty of their hireling crimes,
> The servile, mercenary Swiss of rhymes?
> Or labour hard the panegyric close,
> With all the venal soul of dedicating Prose?

At the beginning of his poem *The Brigs of Ayr,* Burns follows the rules of Classical and Neo-Classical poetry in that he dedicates the poem to a patron, in this instance to John Ballantyne of Ayr. What commands attention, however, is the pose struck by the poet, a posture he maintains in preface, poem and letter, that of the ploughman bard. Hear him as the Cincinnatus of Caledonia answering his own rhetorical question in his rustic simplicity:

> No! though his artless strains he rudely sings,
> And throws his hand uncouthly o'er the strings,
> He glows with all the spirit of the Bard,
> Fame, honest fame, his great, his dear reward.

This is the poet for whose world-wide annual celebration one seeks to account. On January 25th, all over the globe, men and women get together in Burns Clubs, Scottish Societies, country clubs and university Faculty Clubs to eat haggis and drink whisky in honour of a

Scottish farmer who lived over two hundred years ago. Countless special suppers are held, countless haggis are ritualistically slaughtered, and countless panegyrics are delivered in memory of Burns, yet no other Scottish or English poet, not even Shakespeare, is accorded such world-wide honour on his birthday, and this phenomenon demands explanation.

It seems to me that at the heart of the Burns mystique there lies a twin riddle. First, how comes it that Burns has so totally eclipsed all the other poets his homeland has produced and has so completely transcended in the popular mind all Scotland's other heroes such as Robert the Bruce or William Wallace or Bonnie Prince Charlie to become so quintessentially Scotland's eternal representative? And second, how comes it that Robert Burns is, for all that Scottishness, so *universally* admired that on his birthday there are Burns Suppers all over the world in a confusion of languages and dialects second only to that of the Tower of Babel?

For proof of the existence of the twin riddle one need look no further than the *Aberdeen Press and Journal* of Monday, January 14th, 1980 and its article entitled 'Looking at Burns through Red-tinted glasses . . .';

> Every year on Burns Day, January 25, haggis is eaten and whisky drunk not only at Montrose and Macduff but also in Moscow and Murmansk. And each year there is a meeting of East and West in Moscow when a party of Burns devotees from many parts of Scotland visit Russia to toast the memory of Rabbie Burns with fellow enthusiasts from the USSR at a traditional Burns Supper.

Apparently the 1979 affair was filmed by a crew from Grampian-TV and their programme was to be televised on Burns Day, 1980:

> The programme is bound to make fascinating viewing, recording such memorable moments as Russian children singing 'Comin Through the Rye' in a recognisably Scottish accent, and at the Burns Supper itself, Russians and Scots joining in enthusiastic toasts to the Immortal Memory.

There was talk that year of moving or cancelling the Olympic Games, but not the Burns Supper. The Russians took Burns into their hearts long ago, issuing a Bicentenary postage stamp bearing his portrait in 1959 when the British postal authorities did not do so. And on successive January 26th mornings when the Muscovites awaken to that familiar combination of hangover headache and haggis heartburn the Kremlin makes no complaint threatening to our international relations. Indeed, scholarly works on Burns in the Cyrillic alphabet adorn the shelves of the University of Alberta library. It is unfortunate that Dr. Johnson's definition of the after-dinner speaker did not include the requirement that the orator speak Russian, for I should like to read these Russian views on Burns. Alas, I cannot even tell whether or not the introductions contain those remarks which seem indispensable in the West denigrating the drunken, boorish, unlettered Burns Night speakers.

The answer to the twin riddle is not easy to find on this side of the water. One January 25th, for instance, I received a delightfully enigmatic note from an Anglican minister which provided little assistance:

> On this grand and glorious day in the life of every Scotsman, I thought I'd wish you a happy Feast of the Conversion of St. Paul.

This is reminiscent of the BBC announcer some years ago who said, 'The last programme of the evening is "Lighten our darkness, O Lord" except for listeners to the Scottish Home Service.'

An American writer and farmer, Justin Isherwood, suggested in *The Milwaukee Journal* a somewhat meteorological answer to the riddle:

> The significance of Bobbie Burns is less Bobbie Burns than Jan. 25. For there is something about Jan. 25 that needs celebration. Christmas comes too early in the winter and is so laden with tinsel effects that it is ineffectual as a cure against winter. And Feb. 14 is a day for lovers. January is when winter in the midlands is at its worst. The fuel bills are ominously over our heads and the woodpile shrinks at a rate about three weeks short of spring. The January bitterness is compounded by the common cold, by jumper cables, by five-buckle galoshes that fit the foot about as tentatively as the coffin fits the dimension of a man, by long underwear, window drafts and those free plastic windshield scrapers that neatly subdivide the first 10-below morning. All farmers and window watchers are aware on Jan. 25 that the winter solstice came a full month earlier. Yet the earth seems to be unaware of the development — the temperatures are even meaner. This prospect could lure a Northerner toward bitterness and irreverence, were it not for a respite — the observance of Bobbie Burns' birthday.[18]

But the answer is not any easier to find in Scotland than in North America. If anything, the mystery deepens when one first sets one's pilgrim foot again in Scotland in Prestwick Airport. The prodigal returning from exile is greeted by a series of paintings of such Scots worthies as James Watt, Walter Scott, Adam Smith and Robert Burns. Beneath the portrait of Burns is the legend, 'Scotland's National Bard — Ploughman, poet and champion of humanity, his works are loved the world o'er. Born at Alloway 5 miles from here.'

Now, despite all my best efforts at research, Burns's pre-eminence as a ploughman remains a closed book to me. Perhaps it is time the Anglo-Saxon professor turned over the task of the proposal of the Immortal Memory to a colleague in the Faculty of Agriculture, whose jokes might have the necessary boustrophedon quality. I am sure that Burns the practical farmer would know that the best way for a ploughman to start a fire with two small sticks is to make sure that one of them is a match; I am sure that Burns would agree with Mark Twain that 'cauliflower is nothing but cabbage with a college education'; I am sure that Burns would agree with the horror expressed by one ploughman when his friend told him, 'Man, thon shower will dae a hale lot o' guid; it'll fair bring things oot o' the ground.' 'God forbid,' the ploughman exclaimed, 'I've three wives there!' And I am sure that Burns would smile at the annual report recently submitted by a Scottish ploughman: 'The bugs got ma berries, a hail storm ruint ma vegetables, an' the rain spilt ma tatties; bit I'm dae'in fine on the crops the government paid me *nae* tae plant.'

The ploughman pose was one Burns loved to strike, but in assessment of his very complex personality one must not be led astray by the pose into oversimplification. Here is Burns, for instance, introducing his *Commonplace Book 1783-1785:*

> As he was but little indebted to scholastic education, and bred
> at a plough tail, his performances must be strongly tinctured
> with his unpolished rustic way of life; but as I believe they are
> really his own, it may be some entertainment to a curious
> observer of human nature, to see how a plough-man thinks and
> feels, under the pressure of love, ambition, anxiety, grief, with
> the like cares and passions, which, however diversified by the
> modes and manners of life, operate pretty much alike, I believe,
> on all the species.

Yet this is not quite how your every-day ploughman expresses himself, any more than are the following lines from the Dedication to the Edinburgh Edition of 1787:

The Poetic Genius of my country found me, as the prophetic bard
Elijah did Elisha — at the PLOUGH; and threw her inspiring
mantle over me. She bade me sing the loves, the joys, the rural
scenes and rural pleasures of my native soil, in my native tongue:
I tuned my wild, artless notes, as she inspired . . . I was bred to
the plough, and am independent.

The famous letter to Dr. John Moore (Mauchline, August 2nd, 1787)
repeats these claims:

> We lived very poorly: I was a dexterous ploughman, for my age;
> and the next eldest to me was a brother (Gilbert) who could drive
> the plough very well, and help me to thrash the corn . . . At the
> plough, scythe, or reap-hook, I feared no competitor.

The claims are repeated to Sir John Whitefoord (Edinburgh, December 1st, 1786):

> For my part, I thank Heaven, my star has been kinder; learning
> never elevated my ideas above the peasant's shed, and I have an
> independent fortune at the plough-tail.

And in Edinburgh high society Burns would indulge his sense of the
dramatic to the full when playing the role of the ploughman-poet.
How essentially theatrical is the stance adopted when describing his
dining with a lord in *Lines on Meeting With Lord Daer*:

> This wot all ye whom it concerns,
> I, rhymer Rab, alias Burns,
> October twenty-third,
> A ne'er to be forgotten day!
> Sae far I sprachl'd up the brae,
> I dinner'd wi' a Lord. .
>
> But, O! for Hogarth's magic pow'r,
> To shew Sir Bardie's willyart glowr,
> An' how he star'd an' stammer'd!
> When goavan's he'd been led wi' branks,
> An' stumpan' on his ploughman shanks,
> He in the parlour ham mer'd.

Some have been deceived by the pose. Lockhart speaks of Burns as 'having forced his way among them from the plough-tail at a single stride' and Henry Mackenzie referred to him as a 'Heaven-taught ploughman'; his review of the Kilmarnock edition in *The Lounger* read, in part, 'with what uncommon penetration and sagacity this Heaven-taught ploughman, from his humble and unlettered station, has looked upon men and manners.'[19] But there is much more to Burns than the pose held before the *literati* of the time, as Sir Walter Scott was quick to point out. Recounting the occasion when as a lad of fifteen he drew himself to the attention of Burns in the home of Professor Ferguson by being able to identify for Burns the lines below a Banbury print as Langhorne's, Scott goes on to give a striking verbal portrait of the lion of Edinburgh society:

> His person was strong and robust: his manner rustic, not clownish; a sort of dignified plainness and simplicity, which received part of its effect perhaps from one's knowledge of his extraordinary talents. His features are represented in Mr Nasmyth's picture, but to me it conveys the idea that they are diminished as if seen in perspective. I think his countenance was more massive than it looks in any of the portraits. I would have taken the poet, had I not known what he was, for a very sagacious country farmer of the old Scotch school — i.e. none of your modern agriculturists, who keep labourers for their drudgery, but the *douce gudeman* who held his own plough. There was a strong expression of sense and shrewdness in all his lineaments; the eye alone, I think, indicated the poetical character and temperament. It was large and of a dark cast, and glowed (I say literally *glowed*) when he spoke with feeling or interest. I never saw such another eye in a human head, though I have seen the most distinguished men in my time. His conversation expressed perfect self-confidence, without the slightest presumption. Among the men who were the most learned of their time and country, he expressed himself with perfect firmness, but without the least intrusive forwardness; and when he differed in opinion, he did not hesitate to express it firmly, yet at the same time with modesty.[20]

This is not only a ploughman, then, that like Chaucer's 'had ylad of dong ful many a fother' but a ploughman with presence, a ploughman with a fine education, a ploughman poet with enough sense to follow his heart and his Muse rather than accept the advice of the admiring Edinburgh *literati* which would have forced him into the mould of a second-rate copier of English Augustan aesthetics. Thankfully, Burns was capable of better writing than the gaucherie which informs the Spenserian stanzas of *The Cotter's Saturday Night*, and he is more than just another Shenstone.

Ben Jonson could charge the English bard 'thou hadst small Latin, and less Greek' with no more justification than one could level the same charge at Burns. A glance at Burns's letters dispels the notion that the ploughman was ill-educated. His letter to John Murdoch (Lochlee, January 15th, 1783) reads in part as follows:

> In the matter of books, indeed, I am very profuse. My favorite authors are of the sentimental kind, such as *Shenstone*, particularly his *Elegies; Thompson; Man of Feeling*, a book I prize next to the Bible; *Man of the World; Sterne*, especially his *Sentimental Journey; McPherson's Ossian* &c. These are the glorious models after which I endeavour to form my conduct.

The letter to John Moore (Mauchline, August 2nd, 1787) adds to the above list:

> . . . *Pope's Works*, some plays of *Shakespeare, Tull and Dickson on Agriculture, The Pantheon, Locke's Essay on the Human Understanding, Stackhouse's History of the Bible, Justice's British Gardener's Directory, Bayle's Lectures, Allan Ramsay's Works, Taylor's Scripture Doctrine of Original Sin, A Select Collection of English Songs, and Hervey's Meditations* . . .

And his letter to Mrs. Dunlop (Mauchline, May 4th, 1788) shows his acquaintance with the classics:

> Dryden's *Virgil* has delighted me. I do not know whether the critics will agree with me, but the Georgics are to me by far the best of Virgil . . . I own I am disappointed in the *Éneid*. Faultless correctness may please, and does highly please, the lettered critic: but to that awful character I have not the most distant pretensions. I do not know whether I do not hazard my pretensions to be a critic of any kind, when I say that I think Virgil, in many instances, a servile copier of Homer. If I had the *Odyssey* by me, I could parallel many passages where Virgil has evidently copied, but by no means improved Homer.

This is not your average ploughman as far as reading is concerned, and again the pose must be carefully distinguished from the reality. As Scott testifies, Burns could hold his own in conversation with the most learned in the land, and it is not for any false rustic 'simplicity' that Burns is venerated internationally. Yet to tell the posed from the genuine is not always easy, perhaps because Burns in part deceived himself by sometimes assuming a mantle that fitted his shoulders falsely. Not everyone would agree with my view that the ploughman pose flaws *The Cotter's Saturday Night* with overdone rustic posturing or that the avowedly patriotic poems such as *Scots Wha Hae* or *Caledonia* do not ring true and do not contain the best of Burns. One's only guide in assessment of this quandary is ultimately the heart.

To test this, consider first the final stanza of *Caledonia* with its rather precious 'proof' of Scottish destiny based on Pythagoras' theorem (the 47th of Euclid):

> Thus bold, independant, unconquer'd and free,
>   Her bright course of glory for ever shall run;
> For brave Caledonia immortal must be,
>   I'll prove it from Euclid as clear as the sun:
> Rectangle-triangle the figure we'll chuse,
>   The Upright is Chance, and old Time is the Base;
> But brave Caledonia's the Hypotenuse,
>   Then, Ergo, she'll match them, and match them always.

This patriotic drivel is not the best of Burns, by any stretch of the imagination, but is rather of the same order as the old Canadian joke about the Red Indian chief with three wives in his tent. One wife slept on a buffalo skin, the second on a hippopotamus skin and the third on an antelope skin. In due time, all three gave birth; the wife on the buffalo skin had a baby boy, the wife on the hippopotamus skin had twins (a boy and a girl) and the wife on the antelope skin had a little girl. Which simply goes to prove that the squaw on the hippopotamus is equal to the sum of the squaws on the other two hides.

One can learn a great deal more about the essential Burns, the national poet of Scotland and the the poet of universal appeal from the following stanza, whose tone is untrammeled by posing:

> Ye see yon birkie ca'd, a lord,
>   Wha struts, and stares, and a' that,
> Though hundreds worship at his word,
>   He's but a coof for a' that.

> For a' that, and a' that,
> His riband, star and a' that,
> The man of independant mind,
> He looks and laughs at a' that.

The ploughman pose intrudes at the start of the poem *To Miss Ferrier* with the claim that Edinburgh is a finer site for the seat of the Muses than any classical aspirant to that title:

> Nae Heathen Name shall I prefix,
> Frae Pindus or Parnassus;
> Auld Reekie dings them a' to sticks
> For rhyme-inspiring Lasses.

> Jove's tunefu' Dochters three times three
> Made Homer deep their debtor;
> But, gien the body half an e'e,
> Nine Ferriers wad done better.

And this poem is supposedly a letter enclosing Burns's *Elegy on the Death of Sir James Hunter Blair*. The lady is paid a compliment whose tone is extravagant and under the circumstances perhaps inappropriate, a tone worlds apart from that of the poem Burns wrote to welcome his wife to his home:

> O were I on Parnassus hill;
> Or had o' Helicon my fill;
> That I might catch poetic skill,
>   To sing how dear I love thee.
> But Nith maun be my Muses well,
> My Muse maun be thy bonie sell;
> On Corsincon I'll glowr and spell,
>   And write how dear I love thee.

In this example an extra quality is added to the laughter to make the tone genuine, and that quality is love.

The genuine Burns is not found in spurious comparisons with Theocritus and Bion or in the ploughman stumping on his rustic shanks and hammering into the parlour of Edinburgh society. The world would not honour such a poet over two hundred years after his death

with an annual dinner. No, the poet who commands universal esteem
every January speaks in a tongue far different from that suggested by
the pose one finds in biography and autobiography. The ploughman
who gave the world the gaucherie of *The Cotter's Saturday Night*
also gave the unique and heaven-sent simplicity of the auld farmer's
New Year salutation to his auld mare, Maggie; of the poem on the
wounded hare; of the poem to a mouse whose home the ploughshare
had just destroyed; of the poem to the mountain daisy falling under
the blade:

> Wee, modest, crimson-tipped flow'r,
> Thou's met me in an evil hour;
> For I maun crush amang the stoure
> Thy slender stem:
> To spare thee now is past my pow'r,
> Thou bonie gem.

The poet shares a common life with the daisy, truly loves the daisy
and what it represents, and shares a common destiny with the daisy:

> Such is the fate of simple Bard,
> On Life's rough ocean luckless starr'd!
> Unskilful he to note the card
> Of prudent Lore,
> Till billows rage, and gales blow hard,
> And whelm him o'er!

This tender side of the ploughman-poet is the facet of his art which,
less fostered by his legend than the others, gives him poetic and phil-
osophical strength. This may, indeed, be the key to the twin riddle of
Burns — a universal tenderness arising from a unique mixture of
laughter and love.

> Gie me ae spark o' Nature's fire,
> That's a' the learning I desire;
> Then tho' I drudge thro' dub an' mire
> At pleugh or cart,
> My Muse, tho' hamely in attire,
> May touch the heart.

5

Where human weakness has come short

There was a lad was born in Kyle,
But what na day o' what na style,
I doubt it's hardly worth the while
To be sae nice wi' Robin.
Robin was a rovin' Boy,
Rantin' rovin', rantin' rovin';
Robin was a rovin' Boy,
Rantin' Rovin' Robin.

Our monarch's hindmost year but ane
Was five-and-twenty days begun,
'Twas then a blast o' Janwar' Win'
Blew hansel in on Robin.

Burns's Birthplace, Alloway

King George II died in 1760, which makes the date given in the second stanza of *Rantin' Rovin' Robin* work out to Burns's birthday, 'January 25th, 1759, the date of my Bardship's vital existence . . .' The autobiographical poem commemorates the local tradition that the poet's father, William Burness, spurring his horse through storm, dub and mire to fetch the doctor, took pity on a mendicant carlin by the swollen waters of the River Doon and helped her across the torrent. The old woman later uttered over the newborn baby in his cradle in the rough clay cottage at Alloway the prophecy now enshrined in the poem:

> The Gossip keekit in his loof,
> Quo' scho wha lives will see the proof,
> This waly boy will be nae coof,
>   I think we'll ca' him Robin.

> He'll hae misfortunes great and sma',
> But ay a heart aboon them a';
> He'll be a credit till us a',
>   We'll a' be proud o' Robin.

Robin's life was short: January 25th, 1759 to July 21st, 1796, only 37 years. And it was a hard life by any standards, savage and brutal by modern ones. Its tone was established within a few days of its very beginning, for the blast of January wind that blew hansel in on Robin blew out the gable end of the cottage, forcing Agnes and her baby to seek shelter with a neighbour. The poet's brother Gilbert related the incident to Dr. Currie as follows (Dinning, October 24th, 1800):

When my father built his "clay biggin," he put in two stone-jambs, as they are called, and a lintel, carrying up a chimney in his clay-gable. The consequence was, that as the gable subsided, the jambs, remaining firm, threw it off its centre; and, one very stormy morning, when my brother was nine or ten days old, a little before daylight, a part of the gable fell out, and the rest appeared so shattered, that my mother, with the young poet, had to be carried through the storm to a neighbour's house, where they remained a week till their own dwelling was adjusted.

The rebuilt cottage stands to this day in Alloway, a shrine for many pilgrims to visit. In 1781 it was sold to the Incorporation of Shoemakers in Ayr for £160 and for a fair portion of the hundred years of their ownership served as a public house. Later, it fell on better times. The Trustees of the Burns Monument (erected 1820-23 near the Brig o' Doon and across the road from the auld haunted kirk) also purchased the clay biggin in 1881 for £4,000 to turn it into a Burns museum. It is complemented now by the fine new Land o' Burns Centre which lies between the church and the cottage, on the opposite side of the main road.

In his nearest approach to an autobiography of his early career, his letter to Dr. John Moore (Mauchline, August 2nd, 1787), Burns offers the following wry account of his humble station:

> I have not the most distant pretensions to assume that character which the pye-coated guardians of escutcheons call a Gentleman. When at Edinburgh last winter, I got acquainted in the Herald's Office; and, looking through that granary of honours, I there found almost every name in the kingdom; but for me,
> "My ancient but ignoble blood
> Has crept thro' scoundrels ever since the flood."
> Gules, Purpure, Argent, &c. quite disowned me.

Those with a taste for irony will appreciate the story of the events of August, 1787, when Burns came as close as he ever did to Gules, Purpure, Argent, &c. In a letter to Currie, Dr. M. Adair describes Burns's being knighted by Mrs. Catherine Bruce of Clackmannan Tower, an aged Jacobite lady descended directly from Robert the Bruce. The two-handed sword which had belonged to Bruce was used to confer the title, and Mrs. Bruce made much of the fact that she as a Jacobite of impeccable lineage 'had a better right to confer that title than *some people*' (the House of Hanover). Justifiably pleased, Burns later described the heraldic coat of arms he would like in a letter to Alexander Cunningham (March 3rd, 1794):

> I am a bit of a herald, and shall give you, *secundum artem*, my arms. On a field, azure, a holly bush, seeded, proper, in base; a shepherd's pipe and crook, saltier-wise, also proper, in chief. On a wreath of the colours, a wood-lark perching on a sprig of bay-tree, proper, for crest. Two mottoes; round the top of the crest, *Wood notes wild;* at the bottom of the shield, in the usual place, *Better a wee bush than nae bield.*

The eldest of the seven children of William Burness and Agnes Brown, the poet was put to work on the land from an early age and as a consequence received a scant formal education from Campbell at Alloway Mill. His father attempted further lessons in the evenings, but Burns was virtually self-schooled through extensive reading in Latin, French and English. The move to Mount Oliphant in 1766 brought some further opportunities; in 1772 the poet attended Dalrymple parish school for a while in the summer months, and the next year spent three weeks in Ayr studying English and French with John Murdoch. 1773 is better known for Burns's first song, whose genesis he describes to John Moore (Mauchline, August 2nd, 1787):

> This kind of life — the cheerless gloom of a hermit, with the unceasing moil of a galley-slave, brought me to my sixteenth year; a little before which period I first committed the sin of Rhyme. You know our country custom of coupling a man and woman together as partners in the labours of harvest. In my fifteenth autumn, my partner was a bewitching creature, a year younger than myself. My scarcity of English denies me the power of doing her justice in that language; but you know the Scottish idiom — she was a *bonnie, sweet, sonsie lass*. In short, she altogether, unwittingly to herself, initiated me in that delicious passion, which, in spite of acid disappointment, gin-horse prudence, and book-worm philosophy, I hold to be the first of human joys, our dearest blessing here below! . . . Among her other love-inspiring qualities, she sung sweetly; and it was her favourite reel, to which I attempted giving an embodied vehicle in rhyme. I was not so presumptuous as to imagine that I could make verses like printed ones, composed by men who had Greek and Latin; but my girl sung a song, which was said to be composed by a small country laird's son, on one of his father's maids, with whom he was in love; and I saw no reason why I might not rhyme as well as he; for, excepting that he could smear sheep, and cast peats, his father living in the moor-lands, he had no more scholar-craft than myself.

The resulting song was *Handsome Nell*, the first of the many songs with which Burns was to steal the heart of the whole world. Proof of his excellence in this regard subsists in the virtually universal acquaintance accorded such songs as *Scots Wha Hae, Auld Lang Syne, Ye Banks and Braes o' Bonie Doon, Ca' The Yowes, Ae Fond Kiss, Bonie Wee Thing, Afton Water, O My Luve's Like a Red, Red Rose, Green Grow the Rashes O* and *The Lea-Rig*.

Summer of 1775 found Burns in Kirkoswald attending Hugh Roger's school and being distracted from his studies by Peggy Thomson. Burns tells John Moore (Mauchline, August 2nd, 1787):

> Here, though I learnt to fill my glass, and to mix without fear in a drunken squabble, yet I went on with a high hand with my geometry, till the sun entered Virgo, a month which is always a carnival in my bosom, when a charming *fillette* who lived next door to the school, overset my trigonometry, and set me off at a tangent from the sphere of my studies.

And here one meets the Burns of the Burns Legend, the hard-drinker and the hard-lover of popular account.

In 1785, just after Elizabeth Paton bore his daughter Elizabeth, Burns was enamoured of Jean Armour, daughter of a master mason in Mauchline. Rejection of his suit by Jean's family was followed by the affair with his 'Highland Mary', Mary Campbell, and the birth of the twins Robert and Jean by Jean Armour during the next year. 1787 finds an Edinburgh servant named Meg Cameron bringing a paternity suit against the poet, while 1788 finds Burns very active in service of Cupid — the love affair with Agnes McLehose (Clarinda) is followed by the poet's marriage to Jean Armour after she bears him twin daughters who do not survive and before Jenny Clow, another Edinburgh servant, bears him a son. In 1789 Francis Wallace Burns is born to Jean; in 1791 a daughter Elizabeth is born to Anna Park and William Nicol Burns is born to Jean; in 1792 Burns makes friends with Mrs. Walter (Maria) Riddell and Jean bears him Elizabeth Riddell Burns. Etc., etc. Stated thus baldly, the more prominent affairs of the heart have earned Burns latter-day publicity as some sort of rival to Don Juan or the Marquis de Sade, and biographers dispute whether he was a cynical rake and playboy or a warm-hearted romantic struggling with a moral code which would not make one pause today but in his own age earned him the censure of the Kirk Session. Burns describes himself to Moore as suffering from 'social and amorous madness' and falling victim to 'The Devil, the world and the flesh,' though unrepentant. Telling Moore of that early affair at Kirkoswald with Peggy Thomson, he says, '. . . and the two last nights of my stay in the country, had sleep been a mortal sin, I was innocent;' the next paragraph of the letter begins, 'I returned home, very considerably improved.' The twinkle in the eye is as irresistible to his modern readers as it must have proven to the ladies of his choice.

Looking behind sensationalism to the artistic biography, one finds a crisis in Burns's life in 1786. The previous year produced several of the epistles, *Holy Willie's Prayer, The Cotter's Saturday Night* and *The Jolly Beggars: A Cantata*, and Burns now found poverty and social censure forcing on him publication of a volume of poetry to finance an emigrant passage to Jamaica. He explains his motives to Moore as follows (Mauchline, August 2nd, 1787):

> I gave up my part of the farm to my brother; in truth it was only nominally mine; and made what little preparation was in my power for Jamaica. But, before leaving my native country for ever, I resolved to publish my poems. I weighed my productions as impartially as was in my power; I thought they had merit; and it was a delicious idea that I should be called a clever fellow, even though it should never reach my ears — a poor Negro-driver — or perhaps a victim to that inhospitable clime, and gone to the world of spirits! . . . I was pretty confident my poems would meet with some applause; but, at the worst, the roar of the Atlantic would deafen the voice of censure, and the novelty of West-Indian scenes make me forget neglect.

The famous Kilmarnock Edition was published in some 600 copies, and netted the poet around £20 — enough to save him from having to indent himself to pay the £9 cost of his passage. He was en route for Greenock to embark, heavy of heart, for exile when a prominent Edinburgh critic named Dr. Blacklock joined with his friends in persuading the poet to try his fortunes in Edinburgh with a second and enlarged Edinburgh Edition in 1787. This brought Burns money sufficient to secure his brother Gilbert and the family at Mossgiel, to lease Ellisland farm, 6 miles above Dumfries, and to make Jean Armour his legal wife at last in 1788.

For financial and social security, Burns was awarded the post of excisemen of the district of Dumfries, to which town he moved from Ellisland in 1791. The cynical might assume that making Burns exciseman was like setting a wolf to guard a sheepfold, but the poet persisted in the post from 1788 until 1792, when his political views, so often and so strongly expressed, led to his being denounced to the Excise Board as unpatriotic. Burns's artistic energy was unflagging, however, and he produced much poetry during this period — lyrics to James Johnson's *The Scots Musical Museum* in six volumes, 1787-1803, including *Tam o' Shanter*, and poems for George Thomson's *Select Collection of Original Scottish Airs*.

The physical privations of Burns's earlier years began to assert themselves, however, and all the years of over-work and exposure to the elements in a harsh environment began to tell on the poet's constitution, aided by debts and difficulties. Actual suffering followed an unhappy incident in January of 1796. Lingering at the Globe Tavern, Burns was too tired and heady with intoxication to make his way home; instead, he slept in the snow for several hours and contracted the rheumatic fever of which he was never to be rid. Pathetic attempts to restore his health with changes of air and sea-bathing were brought to an end when the poet sank into delirium and then death from subacute bacterial endocarditis on July 21st, 1796. As Currie has it, 'the sufferings of this great, but ill-fated genius were terminated, and a life was closed in which virtue and passion had been at perpetual variance.' On July 25th, the poet was taken from his last home, Mill Vennel, to St. Michael's Churchyard for burial with military honours by the Gentlemen Volunteers of Dumfries. The original simple grave was later replaced by the mausoleum which now covers the mortal remains of Robert Burns, Scotland's national poet.

Such, then, is the biography of a man prodigal of health and heart, working hard in all sorts of weather and playing hard in all sorts of company. And there with other people the story would end, death writing its usual *finis* to human frailty and casting the forgiving cloak of oblivion over the sins of the flesh. Unhappily, this has not been the case with Burns, whose reputation as drinker and wencher persists in bringing his memory to the attention of sensation-seekers who never read the poetry. It is time to demythologize the biography and stop pretending to be shocked by it. One can read much worse nowadays in any daily newspaper. Burns was no worse than the majority of his contemporaries in his behaviour; the only difference was that he was more in the public eye and, alas, much more fertile. The drinking and wenching have obsessed many since a few years after the poet's death, when George Thomson, Robert Heron, James Maxwell, William Peebles, and James Currie gave publicity to his 'excesses', and since then moralists have condemned and canonizing defenders have excused with equal passion. Here, for instance, is Henry Mackenzie in action:

> Burns, originally virtuous, was seduced by dissipated companions, and after he got into the Excise addicted himself to drunkenness, tho' the rays of his genius sometimes broke throught the mist of his dissipation; but the habit had got too much power over him to be overcome, and it brought him, with a few lucid

intervals, to an early grave. He unfortunately during the greatest part of his life had called, and thought, dissipation *spirit,* sobriety and discretion a *want of it,* virtues too shabby for a man of genius. His great admiration of Fergus(s)on shewed his propensity to coarse dissipation.[21]

A different impression of the poet is given by the Rev. J.A. Carruth:

It is true that Burns had his moral lapses, but he fought against them. He fell and he rose again. One recalls his touching poem, 'Welcome to his love-begotten daughter' . . . One is reminded how St Augustine called his natural son "God-given.' Both men lapsed, both repented, both expressed their repentance in immortal literature.

One of Burns's best friends was the Catholic Bishop, John Geddes, for whom the poet had a high regard. In 1787 Burns wrote of him: 'The first (best) Cleric character I ever saw was a Roman Catholic', though later Burns was to have much help and sympathy from Protestant clergymen also.[22]

Neither of these views of Burns is appropriate, for both are too simplistic; Burns was a much more complicated person than either commentator suggests. The first view of Burns as dissipated drunkard and fornicator fails to explain the tenderness and the gentle humour that characterize the best poems, while the view of Burns as saint awaiting canonization by the Vatican makes insufficient allowance for the bawdy Burns. If comparison must be made with St. Augustine, it is not so much with the author of *The City of God* as with the author of *The Confessions* who shared with Burns the sentiment, 'Oh, Lord, give me chastity and continency, but not yet.' The 'Heaven-taught ploughman' was no saint, and even the most ardent apologist, I suspect, smiles in the east room of the Burns Museum at Alloway to see Burns beaming at him in the two stained glass windows made by Cottier & Co. of London.

That defenders can be at least as passionate as detractors was demonstrated to me following one Immortal Memory several years ago in which I had read a few convivial lines from *The Jolly Beggars: A Cantata* to illustrate one facet of Burns's art. I was chided afterwards by a lady who told me indignantly that there was no place for such dirty talk at a Burns Supper, and my only reply was that we were talking about Robert Burns, after all, and not one of the saints.

A better-balanced picture of the poet comes from David Sillar, the Tarbolton teacher to whom Burns addressed the two *Epistles to Davie*:

> After the commencement of my acquaintance with the bard, we frequently met upon Sundays at church, when, between sermons (services), instead of going with our friends or lasses to the inn, we often took a walk in the fields. In these walks I have frequently been struck by his facility in addressing the fair sex; and many times, when I have been bashfully anxious how to express myself, he would have entered into conversation with them with the greatest ease and freedom; and it was generally a deathblow to our conversation, however agreeable, to meet a female acquaintance. Some of the few opportunities of a noontide walk that a country life allows her laborious sons he spent on the banks of the river, or in the woods in the neighbourhood of Stair, a situation peculiarly adapted to the genius of a rural bard.[23]

Add to this the verbal portrait by Scott of the Edinburgh Burns and a clearer picture emerges of a man neither saint nor sinner but a fascinating individual:

> As for Burns, I may truly say, *Virgilium vidi tantum*. I was a lad of fifteen in 1786-7, when he first came to Edinburgh, but had sense and feeling enough to be much interested in his poetry, and would have given the world to know him. . . .[24]

This is the view of Burns one should retain from the biography, throwing away the rest of the ballyhoo. While he was the climax of the Scottish literary tradition which built up for centuries to find its finest expression in the eighteenth century in Burns and Scott, Robert Burns was also a rugged and fascinating individual, a man of strong feelings, a man of sentiment, a man of sorrow, a man of laughter, a man of love for his neighbour, *a man*.

Actually, Burns has fared remarkably well in his native Scotland. It has been pointed out on the best of authority that a prophet is usually without honour in his own country, and this fate has overtaken other Scottish men of letters. Consider, for example, the sad fate of Thomas Carlyle:

> When Thomas Carlyle was confirmed in Olympus, — and Chelsea, — one of his worshippers went on a pilgrimage to Ecclefechan, Carlyle's native village. Approaching a worthy he asked him to point out Thomas Carlyle's birthplace. 'Yonder's the hoose . . .

Ceryl's hoose,' he said, giving the local pronunciation. 'Bit I never heerd tell o' Tam Ceryl daein' onything byordinar. John, they say, is a doctor in Lunnon, but they're no that kenspeckle. To my mind, the pick o' the bunch is Sandy; he's the best breeder o' white pigs on this side o' Lockerbie.' That was hero-worship, though of a Gaderene sort.[25]

The question that is really being raised is whether or not inspired artists can be expected to fit into regular society without making that society uncomfortable. Lord Bertrand Russell used to argue that society should pay its poets a vagabond wage, give them Arts Council grants for subsistence and let them alone to live their extraordinary lives and write. That Burns was well aware of the unusual social status accorded to poets is clear in his letter to Miss Alexander (Mossgiel, November 18th, 1786) in which he writes, 'Poets are such outré beings, so much the children of wayward fancy and capricious whim, that I believe the world generally allows them a larger latitude in the laws of propriety, than the sober sons of judgment and prudence.' Similar sentiments were well expressed about thirty years ago when John Moore proposed the toast to the Immortal Memory in an Edinburgh club:

In our imperfect world poets are indeed safer dead. For whether we like it or not they are not as a rule the kind of people whose company the more respectable members of society can enjoy. Poets are haunted, tormented, plagued like Tom o' Bedlam with 'a host of furious fancies'; they are frequently unhappy and they rarely make good husbands; they are often drunken, frequently dishonest, and generally poor. If you read the Dictionary of National Biography you will find that the biographies of about seven out of ten of our best poets end in alliterative gloom with something like this: *His last days were darkened by debts and drink, or His end was clouded by creditors and catchpoles.* I don't know exactly what a catchpole was: his modern equivalent is doubtless an Income Tax Collector. Anyhow, the point I want to make is that if we expect our poets to be consistently 'good citizens' or 'respectable members of society' we don't deserve poets; because we haven't begun to understand the restlessness and the rage, the passion and the pity, out of which poetry springs.[26]

One point that must be added is that poets upset their audiences by developing, changing, finding consistency a debatable virtue, and writing verse of variable quality. Just as the real Burns has to be quarried from the biography, so the best poetry has to be mined like gold from the dross of the bad poetry one must admit that he penned. A recent biographer, Hugh Douglas, has put the matter succinctly:

> Today . . . affection for Burns has grown into a cult, a kind of worship, which, for many Burnsians, permits no whisper of criticism. And that is a pity, for Burns was neither a man nor a poet in pure black and white. His was a life of a hundred shades of grey, and his poetry ranged from the hastily tossed-off, topical piece to gems in the Scottish tongue. There can be no heights without hollows, no greatness without lesser moments, and the truth about Burns lies somewhere between the Victorian's sore sinner and the idolator's demigod. In short, Burns was a human being who, if he lived his life over again, would order it very differently — and the result would be very much the same![27]

A few days after Burns's decease, Maria Riddell published a *Memoir* in the Dumfries newspaper in which she wrote as follows:

> Besides, the frailties that cast their shade over splendor of superior merit are more conspicuously glaring than where they are the attendants of mere mediocrity; it is only on the gem we are disturbed to see the dust. The pebble may be soiled, and we never regard it. The eccentric intuitions of Genius too often yield the soul to the wild effervescence of desires always unbounded, and sometimes equally dangerous to the repose of others as fatal to its own.[28]

While it would be very wrong of me to impute motives, I do think it fair to say that if any there be who attend Burns Suppers because of the legend they will be disappointed. Whether it be the sinner or the saint whom they seek, they will not find him. Legends come coloured in glaring and stark hues, but anyone familiar with the real Scotland and the real Scottish people will know that their faithful depiction requires rather a palette of a myriad subtle pastel shades. The genuine Robert Burns is too complex a personality to fit comfortably into the Procrustean bed of either extreme category.

The real Robert Burns can be found, of course. One can get a fair idea of what he looked like from Alexander Nasmyth's bust portrait of 1787, commissioned by William Creech for the Edinburgh Edition; from Nasmyth's repetition of the bust portrait as the head for the full-figure painting he supplied in 1827-8 for Lockhart's life of Burns; from Archibald Skirving's 'keel' or chalk drawing based on the Nasmyth bust portrait and praised by Scott as 'the only good portrait of Burns'; from Alexander Reid's water-colour miniature painted on ivory a year before the poet's death and hailed by Burns as 'the most remarkable likeness of what I am at this moment that I ever think was taken of anybody'; from the C.M. Hardie painting of the meeting of Burns and Scott at Sciennes Hill House, the Edinburgh home of Professor Adam Ferguson; and from W.B. Johnstone's 'Sibbald's Circulating Library' of 1786 showing the literary scions of Edinburgh in the bookseller's shop. Burns seems tall and sturdy, and the handsome features are neither cherubic nor coarsened by dissipation. The eyes are as Scott described them, and their appraising gaze is frank, yet gentle; this is a man who would always look his fellow in the eye.

One can hear the real Burns in live, recorded or televised performances by his skilled interpreters. The fine singing of his songs by artists of the calibre of Kenneth McKellar and Bill McCue cannot but move the listener. John Cairney's portrayal of the poet is also rather fine; my only caveat is that sometimes I seem to detect an aggressive, almost abrasive quality I should not ascribe to Burns — otherwise, the Cairney performances are masterly.

And the real Robert Burns is to be found in the poems and in the biography. The reader has to employ his finer sensibilities to separate the man from his legend, but this can be done. One difficulty is, of course, that Burns himself did much to foster the legend, as has been seen in discussion of his rustic ploughman posture, and the reader has therefore to fine-tune his ears and his heart to evaluate each instance of the pose, to distinguish when the tongue is in the cheek and when the heart is full.

A careful reading of the biography shows one neither clear-cut saint nor totally unredeemed sinner, but the usual human mixture of kindness and selfishness, constancy and caprice, charm and beastliness raised to the heights appropriate to genius. Injured pride and sheer pique can show one an idol with feet of clay dealing harshly with poor old Mrs. Oswald of Auchencruive; unselfishness and warmth show one Burns taking in the family of his Uncle Robert following that worthy's death and permitting them to stay in Ellisland as long as necessary, whatever the financial problems caused thereby. The volatile quality in his personality would lead Burns to quarrel sooner or later with those he befriended, but while they were his friends he would deny them nothing of his possessions or of himself. The bad temper that led to ill-judged extempore outbursts such as his *Lines on Viewing Stirling Palace* is balanced by the tenderness that led to such wonderful lyrics as the poem *To A Mouse.* A complex man, a product of his age, physical circumstances and country, living more intensely than most others the common life torn between the extremes of sinner and saint as is the common weal of poets. Byron makes the same claim in *Childe Harold's Pilgrimage:*

> 'Tis to create, and in creating live
> A being more intense, that we endow
> With form our fancy, gaining as we give
> The life we image.

People are more comfortable when saints and sinners alike are dead because they intensify one or other extreme too much for the even tenor of normal lives, and the same is true of the poets whose acting out of the spirit torn by both impulses elevates normal experience to the scale of genius and upsets the average man. In Burns the passion and the sin are there, and this must be admitted and accepted. Don't be the first to cast the stone.

The correct use of the biography is not to build a spurious legend but to cast extra light on the poems where appropriate. A clear example concerns *Lines Written on a Bank-Note*, a note of the Bank of Scotland dated March 1st, 1780:

> Wae worth thy pow'r, thou cursed leaf!
> Fell source of all my woe and grief!
> For lake o' thee I've lost my lass;
> For lake o' thee I scrimp my glass;
> I see the children of Affliction
> Unaided, thro' thy curst restriction;
> I've seen th' Oppressor's cruel smile
> Amid his hapless victim's spoil;
> And for thy potence vainly wish'd
> To crush the Villain in the dust:
> For lake o' thee I leave this much-lov'd shore,
> Never perhaps to greet old Scotland more!

A pleasing conceit, one might think, moving from humour to pathos in the climactic protest that Burns must leave for Jamaica for lack of money. But the biography shows further depth of feeling than is apparent on the surface. In a letter to Mrs. Dunlop, Gilbert Burns recalls his father, William Burness, moving to Edinburgh and sending some money home to his parents:

> Still, however, he endeavoured to spare something for the support of his aged parents; and I recollect hearing him mention his having sent a bank-note for this purpose, when money of that kind was so scarce in Kincardineshire, that they scarcely knew how to employ it when it arrived.

This biographical item adds an extra poignancy to the poem — imagine poverty so hopeless that the use of a bank-note is virtually unknown! Such pathos goes far beyond mere everyday economics, what Wordsworth called 'getting and spending'; such pathos in Burns's experience is a matter quite frankly of life or death. Consider Scott's remark in this context:

> He was much caressed in Edinburgh, but (considering what literary emoluments have been since his day) the efforts made for his relief were extremely trifling.[29]

Or consider the final modern irony — Burns's features adorn the Clydesdale Bank's £5 note.

Such correct use of the biography can illuminate certain aspects of Burns's writings when properly applied as above. Such correct use of the biography when taken along with the relevant poems can help answer the twin riddle of Burns.

Writing in prospect of death, Burns wryly describes his real biography:

> Some drops of joy with draughts of ill between;
> Some gleams of sunshine mid renewing storms . . . .

And Burns speaks more frankly and honestly than his critics and supporters of the contradictory sides of his personality:

> Fain would I say, 'Forgive my foul offence!'
> Fain promise never more to disobey;

> But should my Author health again dispense,
> Again I might desert fair Virtue's way;
> Again in Folly's path might go astray;
> Again exalt the brute and sink the man.

His final *apologia pro vita sua* is disarming in its simplicity and sincerity, giving the lie to the legend through admission of human weakness and recognition of the only possible answer to it:

> O Thou unknown, Almighty Cause
> Of all my hope and fear!
> In whose dread Presence, ere an hour,
> Perhaps I must appear!

> If I have wander'd in those paths
> Of life I ought to shun;
> As Something, loudly, in my breast,
> Remonstrates I have done;

> Thou know'st that Thou hast formed me
> With Passions wild and strong;
> And list'ning to their witching voice
> Has often led me wrong.

> Where human weakness has come short,
> Or frailty stept aside,
> Do Thou, All-Good, for such Thou art,
> In shades of darkness hide.

> Where with intention I have err'd,
> No other plea I have,
> But, Thou art good; and Goodness still
> Delighteth to forgive.

Let all forget the Nithsdale Horace and go in search of Scotland's national poet and the bard of universal appeal. Let the legend finally rest.

6
Hey tutti taiti

What needs this din about the town o' Lon'on?
How this new Play, and that new Sang is comin?
Why is outlandish stuff sae meikle courted?
Does Nonsense mend, like Brandy, when imported —
Is there nae Poet, burning keen for Fame,
Will bauldly try to gie us Plays at hame?
For Comedy abroad he need na toil,
A Knave an' Fool are plants of ev'ry soil;
Nor need he hunt as far as Rome or Greece,
To gather matter for a serious piece;
There's themes enow in Caledonian story,
Wad show the Tragic Muse in a' her glory.

Is there no daring Bard will rise and tell
How glorious Wallace stood, how hapless fell?
Where are the Muses fled, that should produce
A drama worthy of the name of Bruce?

This *Prologue for Mr. Sutherland's Benefit Night, Dumfries* was
written for the manager of the Dumfries Theatre, and serves now to
raise the important question of Burns's patriotic poetry. Is Burns the
poet of universal appeal and the national poet of Scotland necessarily
to be identified with Burns the partriot and politician, or do the roots
of his appeal run deeper than an emotional rendering of *Scots Wha
Hae?* Dare we give full credence to Burns's letter to Mrs. Dunlop
(Edinburgh, March 22nd, 1787:

> The appellation of a Scottish bard is by far my highest pride; to
> continue to deserve it is my most exalted ambition. Scottish scenes
> and Scottish story are the themes I could wish to sing. I have no
> dearer aim than to have it in my power, unplagued with the routine
> of business, for which, heaven knows! I am unfit enough, to make
> leisurely pilgrimages through Caledonia; to sit on the fields of her

battles; to wander on the romantic banks of her rivers; and to muse by the stately towers or venerable ruins, once the honoured abodes of her heroes.

Robert Burns is *not* Scotland's national poet because, as jealous Englishmen assert, he is Scotland's *only* poet; she can also boast Scott, Dunbar, Henryson, Fergusson, Ramsay, Hogg. He is *not* Scotland's national poet because of his long and intimate acquaintance with women — although that made him a great philosopher. He is *not* the universal poet of January 25th because of his long and intimate acquaintance with the Devil — although that made him a great theologian and a great drinker. *Nor* is he the Scottish ambassador *par excellence* because Scotland's history has a dearth of heroes — William Wallace, Robert the Bruce, Rob Roy MacGreagor and Bonnie Prince Charlie provide material sufficient for even the most rabid romantic.

I do not think it can seriously be maintained that Burns is Scotland's national poet simply because of his use of the Scottish vernacular as the vehicle of some of his verse, for in this, too, he is by no means unique. It cannot be Burns's use of the Scots tongue that earns his memory such widespread celebration, for so much of what he said cannot be translated into English, let alone more alien tongues; I am amused at New Year to watch the television broadcast of revellers in Times Square linking arms and singing *Auld Lang Syne* when I know most of them cannot tell 'a right guid-willie waught' from 'a daimen icker in a thrave'. And I dearly wish I could read Russian to see just what the Kremlin makes of Burns's letter to his friend William Nicol, master of the High School, Edinburgh (Carlisle, June 1st, or May 39th [sic], 1787):

> I'm sitten down here, after seven and forty miles ridin, e'en as forjesket and forniaw'd as a forfoughten cock, to gie you some notion o' my landlowper-like stravaguin sin the sorrowfu' hour that I sheuk hands and parted wi' auld Reekie.
>
> My auld, ga'd Gleyde o' a meere has huchyall'd up hill and down brae, in Scotland and England, as teugh and birnie as a vera devil wi' me. — It's true, she's as poor's a Sang-maker and as hard's a kirk, and tipper-taipers when she taks the gate first like a Lady's gentlewoman in a minuwae, or a hen on a het girdle, but she's a yauld, poutherie Girran for a' that; and has a stomach like Willie Stalker's meere that wad hae digeested tumbler-wheels, for she'll whip me aff her five stimparts o' the best aits at a down-

sittin and ne'er fash her thumb. — When ance her ringbanes and spavies, her crucks and cramps, are fairly soupl'd, she beets to, beets to, and ay the hindmost hour the tighest. — I could wager her price to a thretty pennies that, for twa or three wooks ridin at fifty mile a day, the deil-sticket a five gallopers acqueesh Clyde and Whithorn could cast saut in her tail.

I hae dander'd owre a' the kintra frae Dumbar to Selcraig, and hae forgather'd wi' monie a guid fallow, and monie a weel-far'd hizzie. — I met wi' twa dink quines in particular, ane o' them a sonsie, fine fodgel lass, baith braw and bonie; the tither was a clean-shankit, straught, tight, weel-far'd winch, as blythe's a lint -white on a flowerie thorn, and as sweet and modest's a new blawn plumrose in a hazle shaw. — They were baith bred to mainers by the beuk, and onie ane o' them has as muckle smeddum and rumblegumtion as the half o' some Presbytries that you and I baith ken. — They play'd me sik a deevil o' a shavie that I daur say if my harigals were turn'd out, ye wad see twa nicks i' the heart o' me like the mark o' a kail-whittle in a castock.

While this is not an overdrawn picture of the Edinburgh Doric of Burns's time, even the most avid Burns supporter is forced to admit that this is hardly a universal language.

The language of the Scot reflects much of what is essential to the Scottish soul — earthiness, directness, practicality, starkness, harshness tempered on occasion with the warmth of lyricism. The Scot is always sensitive to the nuances of language; take, for instance the tale of the little boy coming home from school and saying to his mother, 'I didna like school the day — I wish ah hadna goed.' 'Na, na,' corrected his mother, 'You mean you wish to Goad ye hadna went!' And just as in the book of *Judges* Jepthah used the test-word 'shibboleth' to distinguish the fleeing Ephraimites from his own Gileadite followers, so the Scots require aspirants to true nationality to articulate 'It's a braw, bricht, moon-licht nicht the nicht the noo.' They might just as well demand the reading aloud of the letter of Burns to Nicol which has just been considered.

This is not, of course, Burns's only voice. He could command perfect English when he chose to do so, as in this flyting (of 1791?) addressed to a fellow Scot aping the English school of poetry:

> Thou Eunuch of language: thou Englishman, who never was south of the Tweed: thou servile echo of fashionable barbarisms: thou quack, vending the nostrums of empirical elocution: thou

marriage-maker between vowels and consonants, on the Gretna-green of caprice: thou cobbler, botching the flimsy socks of bombast oratory: thou blacksmith, hammering the rivets of absurdity: thou butcher, embruing thy hands in the bowels of orthography: thou arch-heretic in pronunciation: thou pitch-pipe of affected emphasis: thou carpenter, mortising the awkward joints of jarring sentences: thou squeaking dissonance of cadence: thou pimp of gender: thou Lyon Herald to silly etymology: thou antipode of grammar: thou executioner of construction: thou lingual confusion worse confounded: thou scape-gallows from the land of syntax: thou scavenger of mood and tense: thou murderous accoucheur of infant learning: thou ignis fatuus, misleading the steps of benighted ignorance: thou pickle-herring in the puppet-show of nonsense: thou faithful recorder of barbarous idiom: thou persecutor of syllabication: thou baleful meteor, foretelling and facilitating the rapid approach of Nox and Erebus.

Just try getting your tongue round that after a few drinks!

One is forced to the conclusion that Burns's universal popularity cannot be ascribed to his writing in braid Scots. Other native Scots poets used the vernacular, from Barbour, Henryson and Dunbar through Hogg, Galt and Scott to MacDiarmid; and besides, Burns could write most cleverly in standard, literary English when it suited his purpose to do so. Burns was master of the entire range of language from the humblest Doric to the most learned English, and could match his vehicle to his tenor ideally. And the tenor is, of course, where one finds the essential Robert Burns, where one finds the laughter and the love which in combination give him his unique appeal.

The more one studies Burns, the more an apparently straightforward subject becomes complicated. Trying to understand the universal appeal of Burns is like putting one's finger on a blob of mercury — the harder one tries, the more elusive becomes success. The more obvious and popular responses are not ultimately part of the answer at all. Just as one has to set aside over-emphasis on the biography and over-emphasis on Burns's use of the Scots vernacular, so, I think, one must discount the patriotic and political poetry. Burns is not Scotland's national poet because he wrote poems full of patriotic fervour, such as *Scots Wha Hae*; such poems are dangerous, for they do *not* show the essence of Burns. There is a false feel to such poems, something about them which does not ring true. The problem is that patriotism is part of politics and politics is the facet of human endeavour that changes most rapidly. This is to say, in effect, that any account of politics the moment it is written becomes a period piece, and that poetry with a political bias does not wear well. It is doubly unfortunate, then, that patriotic sentiments expressed in such political poems can sound trite and clichéd; *The Cotter's Saturday Night* considered from this point of view is a very bad poem.

A rehashing of yesterday's politics is even less exciting than eating yesterday's leftovers and as relevant to today's experience as an empty beer can. Discussion of the politics of a past age leaves one's audience agog with apathy, and nothing can be duller than a past century's political verse. Burns's political poetry is no exception, alas, and this aspect of his writing has not worn well. The Act of Union of 1707 left the Scottish Whig party divided against itself, with some of its adherents become Jacobite and some allied to the Revolution Whigs of England. Such a dual standard is found in the poetry of Burns, for his disapproval of the later Stuarts and his demand for democracy are balanced by his Scottish nationalist fervour and his sentimental support of the Jacobite cause. Burns the revolutionary hailed the French Revolution with Wordsworth and Coleridge, while Burns the Jacobite saw salvation in the idea of turning the clock back to Stuart absolutism. In addition, Burns's championship of the common man and his investing the life of the poor with dignity have been taken by a later age to indicate that he was a communist. Now, one could not hold *all* the political stances of varying hues which have been attributed to Burns — Jacobite, Jacobin, Whig, Revolutionary, Republican, Communist, Royalist, Scottish Nationalist — and while there are no doubt those who come to the poet for this political affiliation or that, it is most honest to reflect that history has rolled on its Juggernaut way two centuries since Burns and the burning questions of his day are now cold ashes. The various political poses in Burns's poetry are as remote from the real Burns as the rustic ploughman stance investigated earlier.

Asked if Scotland has her own national anthem, the average man would not be so likely to answer *Scotland the Brave* or *The Flower of Scotland* as to reply *Scots Wha Hae*. Burns wrote the song in 1793, and sent it to Thomson with the following note (September, 1793:

> There is a tradition, which I have met with in many places in Scotland, that [the old air, 'Hey tutti taiti,'] was Robert Bruce's march at the battle of Bannockburn. This thought, in my solitary wanderings, warmed me to a pitch of enthusiasm on the theme of Liberty and Independence, which I threw into a kind of Scottish

ode, fitted to the air that one might suppose to be the gallant Royal Scot's address to his heroic followers on that eventful morning.

Thomson did not like the tune, however, and confirmed Burns's fears on the matter by printing the words with the tune 'Lewie Gordon.' Only in 1801 did Thomson set the words to 'Hey tutti taiti', and even then offered alternative lyrics, Lady Nairne's *The Land o' the Leal* and a Jacobite song *Weel May We a' Be*.

There was nothing new about the tune. 'Hey tutti taiti' is an ancient trumpet tune which may have been centuries old at the time of Bannockburn. Tradition has it that Joan of Arc's Scots archers played it on the Maid's entrance into Rheims Cathedral, and it was popular in the sixteenth century as an *aubade* beginning, 'Hey, noo the day daws, the joly cock craws'; William Dunbar complains as follows in *To the Merchants of Edinburgh:*

> Your commone menstrallis hes no tone
> Bot 'Now the day dawis', and 'Into Joun' . . .[30]

It was the addition of Burns's fervid words that was new, that transformed the ancient trumpeters' *reveille* into a clarion call for liberty which moved Thomas Carlyle to claim, 'So long as there is warm blood in the heart of Scotchman or man, it will move in fierce thrills under this war-ode; the best, we believe, that was ever written by any pen.'

> Scots, wha hae wi' Wallace bled,
> Scots, wham Bruce has aften led,
> Welcome to your gory bed,
>   Or to victorie.
>
> Now's the day, and now's the hour;
> See the front o' battle lour;
> See approach proud Edward's power,
>   Chains and Slaverie.
>
> Wha will be a traitor-knave?
> Wha can fill a coward's grave?
> Wha sae base as be a Slave?
>   — Let him turn and flie.

> Wha for Scotland's king and law
> Freedom's sword will strongly draw,
> Free-man stand, or Free-man fa',
>   Let him follow me.
>
> By Oppression's woes and pains!
> By your Sons in servile chains!
> We will drain our dearest veins,
>   But they shall be free!
>
> Lay the proud Usurpers low!
> Tyrants fall in every foe!
> Liberty's in every blow!
>   Let us Do — or Die!!!

The singing of these words at a Burns Supper leads to deserved applause, because the marriage of words and tune has an undeniable effect. Yet, if the words be divorced from the music and scrutinized on their own, an artifical and studied quality may be perceived. Part of the problem is linguistic: 'Scots, wha hae' is not authentic Middle Scots, for Bruce would actually have said, 'Scots, *that has* wi' Wallace bled.' And part of the problem lies in the sentiment, for the patriotic fervour is of uncertain application. The victory of 1314 was as stale news in 1793 as Burns's politics are today, and Burns was less concerned with Bannockburn when he wrote the poem as with the current Edinburgh sedition trials and with the glorious dawn of the French Revolution. Liberty in general is the theme, not Scottish nationalism in particular. Note the climax of his description of the battle to Lord Buchan (Dumfries, January 12th, 1794) on sending the earl a copy of the poem:

> Independently of my enthusiasm as a Scotsman, I have rarely met with anything in history which interests my feelings as a man equal with the story of Bannockburn. On the one hand a cruel, but able usurper, leading on the finest army in Europe, to extinguish the last spark of freedom among a greatly-daring and a greatly-injured people; on the other hand, the desperate relics of a gallant nation, devoting themselves to rescue their bleeding country or perish with her. Liberty! thou art a prize truly and indeed valuable, for never canst thou be too dearly bought.

Robert The Bruce Statue, Bannockburn

The poem shares this climax, which is not the expression of specifically Scottish partriotism many mistakenly think it to be. If *Scots
Wha Hae* has value to us today as a political poem, it is because of
the real theme, that of liberty in general and the right of every man
to its enjoyment and privilege. Such, indeed, was the point of the
Declaration of Arbroath when, on April 6, 1320, the nobles, clergy
and commons of Scotland sent to Pope John XXII a noble statement
of their devotion to liberty for all:

> So long as a hundred of us are left alive, we shall never be subject
> to English domination. It is not for glory, nor riches, nor honour
> that we fight, but only for that liberty which no true man relin-
> quishes but with his life.

Patriotism is as honourable an inspiration for poetry as any other,
but its expression can too easily sound trite or perfervid. Control must
be rigorous lest the verse degenerate into jingoism. Burns, alas, does
not always strike the right balance in his political poems. To see the
difference in his approach, compare his stated intentions to the sentiments expressed a hundred years earlier by Andrew Fletcher of
Saltoun:

No inclination is so honourable, nor has anything been so much esteemed in all nations, and ages, as the love of that country and society in which every man is born. And those who have placed their greatest satisfaction in doing good, have accounted themselves happy, or unfortunate, according to the success of their endeavours to serve the interest of their country. For nothing can be more powerful in the minds of men, than a natural inclination and duty concurring in the same disposition.[31]

No such controlled tone characterizes Burns's remarks in his letter to John Moore (Mauchline, August 2nd, 1787):

The two first books I ever read in private, and which gave me more pleasure than any two books I ever read since, were, *The Life of Hannibal,* and *The History of Sir William Wallace.* Hannibal gave my young ideas such a turn, that I used to strut in raptures up and down after the recruiting drum and bag-pipe, and wish myself tall enough to be a soldier; while the story of Wallace poured a Scottish prejudice into my veins, which will boil along there till the floodgates of life shut in eternal rest.

The Scottish prejudice boiling in Burns's veins leads to extravagance of the type encountered in the exposition of Pythagoras' theorem in *Caledonia* and in the fragment *Liberty* sent to Mrs. Dunlop with the following words (Castle Douglas, June 25th, 1794):

The subject is Liberty. You know, my honoured friend, how dear the theme is to me. I design it as an irregular ode for General Washington's birthday . . .

Thee, Caledonia, thy wild heaths among,
Famed for the martial deed, the heaven-taught song,
To thee, I turn with swimming eyes. —
Where is the soul of Freedom fled?

The heroism of Wallace is not to be found in contemporary Scotland:

Shew me that eye which shot immortal hate,
Blasting the Despot's proudest bearing:
Shew me that arm which, nerved with thundering fate,
Braved Usurpation's boldest daring!
Dark-quenched as yonder sinking star,
No more that glance lightens afar;
That palsied arm no more whirls on the waste of war.

That this is overdone can be seen by setting it beside Wordsworth's *Milton*, a poem expressing similar sentiments but with surer handling of the emotions. Again, Burns writing of Scottish patriotism seeks to write really of liberty in general, just as in *Scots Wha Hae*. One cannot but wonder what Washington would have made of the poem.

Robert Bruce fares a little better in the fragmentary *Bruce*, where he is seen as a Scottish Mars, Thor or Zeus controlling the lightning storm:

> His royal visage seamed with many a scar,
> That Caledonian reared his martial form,
> Who led the tyrant-quelling war,
> Where Bannockburn's ensanguined flood
> Swelled with mingling hostile blood,
> Soon Edward's myriads struck with deep dismay,
> And Scotia's troop of brothers win their way.
> (Oh, glorious deed to bay a tyrant's band!
> Oh, heavenly joy to free our native land!)
> While high their mighty chief poured on the
>   doubling storm.[32]

The picture is over-painted. Even the scansion is reminiscent of that of McGonagall.

Burns the Jacobite has no better a sense of balance. Alongside the dewy-eyed sentimentality of *It was A' For our Rightfu' King* and *Charlie, He's My Darling* skulks the epigram Burns wrote after visiting Stirling Palace. On a window of James Wingate's Inn in King Street, Stirling (now the Golden Lion Hotel), Burns scratched these lines with a diamond ring:

> Here Stewarts once in triumph reign'd,
> And laws for Scotland's weal ordain'd;
> But now unroof'd their Palace stands,
> Their sceptre's fall'n to other hands;
> Fallen indeed, and to the earth,
> Whence grovelling reptiles take their birth. —
> The injur'd Stewart-line are gone,
> A Race outlandish fill their throne;
> An idiot race, to honor lost;
> Who know them best despise them most.

This epigram rightly earned the censure of the minister of Gladsmuir, Mr. Hamilton, and to right matters in part Burns wrote himself this mock reproof:

> Rash mortal, and slanderous Poet, the name
> Shall no longer appear in the records of fame;
> Dost not know that old Mansfield, who writes
> like the Bible,
> Says the more 'tis a truth, Sir, the more 'tis
> a libel?

Burns had so misjudged the effect of his sentiments and occasioned so much offence that the next time he visited Stirling he smashed the pane of glass with his riding-whip. He also made the mistake of replying to the minister of Gladsmuir:

> With Esop's lion, Burns says, sore I feel
> Each other blow, but damn that ass's heel!

The Russians have long since taken the political Burns to their hearts for his revolutionary sentiments. Here is an example of what the Russians like in Burns, the description offered in *The Twa Dogs* by the dog Caesar of the great man going to London to attend Parliament:

> Haith lad, ye little ken about it;
> *For Britain's guid*! guid faith! I doubt it.
> Say rather, gaun as Premiers lead him,
> An' saying *aye* or *no*'s they bid him:
> At Operas an' Plays parading,
> Mortgaging, gambling, masquerading:
> Or maybe, in a frolic daft,
> To Hague or Calais takes a waft,
> To make a *tour* an' take a whirl,
> To learn *bon ton* an' see the worl' . . .
> *For Britain's guid*! for her destruction!
> Wi' dissipation, feud an' faction!

I do not think one can find the genuine Burns in the revolutionary verses any more than in the patriotic and Jacobite verses. Nothing yet quoted in this chapter makes Burns Scotland's national poet or the poet of universal appeal. Such poems and letters as those just scanned are dangerous, for they do *not* show the essence of Burns; Burns the political activist rings no truer to one's ears than Burns the rustic ploughman, and Burns is *not* Scotland's national poet because he wrote verses about the Stuarts or verses expressing revolutionary sentiments. It may seem paradoxical that the national bard is not given his accolade for his ostensibly patriotic poetry, but one is forced to the conclusion that he wears the laurel for something deeper than his patriotic veneer. The love and the laughter are wanting from the period-piece poetry of avowed patriotic inspiration.

It is unfortunate that one must include in the condemnation of over-blown Scottish sentimentality *The Cotter's Saturday Night*, for it is perhaps the most popular poem of the Kilmarnock Edition. Eschewing the false notes of the ostensibly political poems, *The Cotter's Saturday Night* sets out to assert eternal Scottishness on surer grounds — the simple dignity of the honest labourer and his sincere devotion. With a wealth of homely detail, Burns paints a verbal portrait of the *echt* Scot, the rustic farmer leading the family worship with a touching reverence:

> The chearfu' Supper done, wi' serious face,
>   They, round the ingle, form a circle wide;
> The Sire turns o'er, with patriarchal grace,
>   The big ha'-Bible, ance his Father's pride:
> His bonnet rev'rently is laid aside,
>   His lyart haffets wearing thin and bare;
> Those strains that once did sweet in Zion glide,
>   He wales a portion with judicious care;
> 'And let us worship God!' he says with solemn air.

This stanza is the emotional heart of the poem, and it has earned widespread praise. William Hazlitt has described the poem as 'a noble and pathetic picture of human manners, mingled with a fine religious awe. It comes over the mind like a slow and solemn strain of music.' And Gilbert Burns confirms to Currie the centrality of the portrait to the poet's inspiration (Mossgiel, April 2nd, 1798; Dinning, October 24th, 1800):

Robert had frequently remarked to me that he thought there was something peculiarly venerable in the phrase, 'Let us worship God,' used by a decent sober head of a family introducing family worship. To this sentiment of the author the world is indebted for the

Cotter's Saturday Night . . . The 'Cotter', in the Saturday Night, is an exact copy of my father in his manners, his family devotion, and exhortations, yet the other parts of the description do not apply to our family.

Yet this masterpiece is seriously flawed by several faults of balance. It is written in a strange and uncomfortable mixture of literary English and couthy Scots dialect which makes the poem at once too pretentious and too patronising in its tone. The quatrain from Gray's *Elegy* which prefaces the poem tells one that Burns is writing in imitation of Gray and other English poets like Goldsmith and Milton who have sought to invest the state of the impoverished with dignity; the imitation, unfortunately, is too close, resulting in heroic dection of a kind which is inappropriate to the subject-matter and which makes Burns sound like a second Shenstone. The poem is written in Spenserian stanzas, a metre too unwieldy for a poem about simplicity and too reminiscent of the works of others who have handled the form more skilfully, from Spenser himself to James Thomson. Further, Burns's attempt to introduce humour into the poem fails, partly because the diction and metre make it too heavy-handed and partly because humour is misplaced in a poem so redolent of elegy. None of these faults afflicts Burns's model, Robert Fergusson's *The Farmer's Ingle*, and readers have to admit that Burns's poem is far less masterly or convincing.

To illustrate the faults to be found with *The Cotter's Saturday Night*, I should like to consider briefly two successive stanzas:

> Is there, in human-form, that bears a heart —
> A wretch! a villain! lost to love and truth!
> That can, with studied, sly, ensnaring art,
> Betray sweet Jenny's unsuspecting youth?
> Curse on his perjur'd arts! dissembling smoothe!
> Are Honour, Virtue, Conscience, all exil'd?
> Is there no Pity, no relenting Ruth,
> Points to the Parents fondling o'er their Child?
> Then paints the ruin'd Maid, and their distraction wild!

> But now the Supper crowns their simple board,
> The healsome Porritch, chief of Scotia's food:
> The soupe their only Hawkie does afford,
> That 'yont the hallan snugly chows her cood:

> The Dame brings forth, in complimental mood,
> To grace the lad, her weel-hain'd kebbuck, fell;
> And aft he's prest, and aft he ca's it guid;
> The frugal Wifie, garrulous, will tell,
> How 'twas a towmond auld, sin' Lint was i' the bell.

The picture of the vile seducer is over-painted. This is the sort of obvious villain whom audiences boo in the Victorian melodrama or *The Perils of Pauline* type of early film, and one can see the thick hair-oil, smell the after-shave. I have not lost my sense of humour so much as Burns has his, for if the poem's tone is modelled on that of Gray's *Elegy* humour is inappropriate and destructive of the overall tone. In addition, the heroic diction inflates the intended humour to something far too aggrandise to be funny; the line separating pathos and bathos is fine, and Burns misjudges here where it is drawn. Since the humour fails, the condemnation of the vile seducer of an innocent young maid becomes hypocritical since it purports to come from Burns of all people. Those who come to Burns Suppers for the biography are prevented only by Gilbert Burns's assurance that 'the other parts of the description do not apply to our family' from taking this to be Burns's self-portrait.

Turning immediately to the following stanza is an experience akin to riding an elevator that descends too fast, for one falls too speedily down the gulf which should separate the studied and heroic diction of high literary English style from the simple and unaffected diction which ought to characterise the lower level of rustic dialect style. Suddenly there is a switch to Scots so broad that editors swamp the reader with glosses for 'Hawkie', 'hallan', 'weel-hain'd kebbuck', 'towmond' and 'sin' Lint was i' the bell', some even feeling that for English readers it is necessary to gloss 'Porritch' and 'chows her cood'. This is like downing a drink which at one moment tastes of whisky and the next tastes of vodka, or like taking part in a conversation in French which suddenly switches to being in German. To see the havoc wreaked on the porritch by the diction and the Spenserian stanza, one has only to recall the *Address to the Haggis* to enter a different world of poetic achievement.

In fine, it may be from scenes like these that old Scotia's grandeur springs, but it is not from poems like this that Burns earns his reputation as Scotland's national poet. The concluding stanza is filled with all the danger signs we have come to recognize:

O Thou! who pour'd the patriotic tide,
   That stream'd thro' great, unhappy Wallace' heart;
Who dar'd to, nobly, stem tryannic pride,
   Or nobly die, the second glorious part:
(The Patriot's God, peculiarly thou art,
   His friend, inspirer, guardian and reward!)
O never, never Scotia's realm desert,
   But still the Patriot, and the Patriot-bard,
In bright succession raise, her Ornament and Guard!

The over-blown diction which likens Wallace's blood to a patriotic tide poured by God is matched by the invocation of God himself as the Muse of patriotic poetry. Here is Burns in his familiar patriot pose, with the story of Wallace pouring a Scottish prejudice in his veins which will boil along there till the flood-gates of life shut in eternal rest. The concluding conceit requires no comment.

The patriot bard is not necessarily to be equated with the national bard, and the patriotic and political poems are *not* at the core of Burns's universal appeal. The real Burns does not subsist in such poems as *The Author's Earnest Cry and Prayer to The Scotch Representatives in the House of Commons* or *My Heart's in the Highlands* but in *The Auld Farmer's New-Year Morning Salutation to his Auld Mare Maggie* and *To A Mouse*. The difference is that the striking of a right balance is effected by the addition of the vital quality I call the laughter of love. The real Burns is to be found in the genuine and heart-felt universal warmth of *Auld Lang Syne* in which the warmth of love for one's fellow-man speaks through the Scottish idiom and dialect to extend the expression of Scottish brotherly affection to embrace all mankind, whatever their individual races or tongues. The real Burns is to be found in the poems which are political in only the broadest sense of the word, not in the narrow chauvinistic or avowedly patriotic sense; the laughter and the love make the *polis* of his best poems *all* mankind and makes their values universal in appeal and application for all that their expression is quintessentially and unmistakably Scottish. In this apparent contradiction lies the key to Robert Burns, for the laughter and the love dissolve all contradiction in the warmth of their universality.

What though on hamely fare we dine,
Wear hoddin grey, and a' that.
Gi'e fools their silks, and knaves their wine,
A Man's a Man for a' that.
For a' that, and a' that,
Their tinsel show, and a' that;
The honest man, though e'er sae poor,
Is king o' men for a' that.

7

Satan, I fear thy sooty claws

> An' now, auld Cloots, I ken ye're thinkan,
> A certain Bardie's rantin, drinkin,
> Some luckless hour will send him linkan
>   To your black pit;
> But, faith! he'll turn a corner jinkan,
>   An' cheat you yet.

Burns Supper orators have to be a hardy lot, for many dangers lie in their path. Besides the usual hecklers and rival orators in the audience, there are, for instance, the Audio-Visual technicians who, upon equipping me with a tie-clip microphone to leave my hands free during the addressing of the haggis, assure me that their high-tension cables have to be connected to my sporran. One learns to tread warily under such circumstances.

Then there are dire warnings from the shade of the departed poet. In Easter of 1981, visiting the Burns Country to take photographs and hoping to interview a few people, I did not tread warily on entering the Burns Cottage at Alloway. A sudden mighty blow in the stomach heralded the bursting of my appendix, and as I was hurried off to emergency surgery I reflected ruefully that perhaps the poet himself had issued a stern admonition to an unskilled aspirant.

Yet these impediments to progress are as nothing compared to my experience over the 1978 Immortal Memory at the University of Alberta Faculty Club. As I rose to propose the toast, the emphasis was placed more than usual on the word 'rose.' Burns wrote wistfully in *To A Louse* a justly famous couplet:

> O wad some Pow'r the giftie gie us
> To see oursels as others see us!

Well, the Pow'r for whom he longed appeared in this latter day in the form of a junta comprising Printing Services and the management of the Club. I have the unique privilege of seeing masel as ithers see me,

I know what my friends and colleagues think of me: they think I'm dead! The advertisement for the evening's celebration read as follows:

ROBBIE BURNS NIGHT

The evening features Piping in the Haggis by Rorri McBlane, Scottish Dancing by the University of Alberta Scottish Country Dance Club, and The Address to the Haggis and Toast to the Immortal Memory of Dr. Raymond Grant.

I was assured that this was an error, the typo to end all typos, but I have read Freud and am not so sure. Several colleagues expressed their sympathy on my passing, however, and Dr. May in Classics wrote to ask if my demise was to be celebrated just that once or if it was to become an annual event.

My first reaction was to deny that I had died and to borrow the obvious quote from Mark Twain, who sent the Associated Press a telegram from Europe which read: 'Your report of my death is somewhat exaggerated.' Then I toyed with the idea of remaining dead after all; I could collect my life insurance and live the life of Old Reilly with it; I could drain the Academic Pension Plan for the next half-century or so; I could quite legitimately refuse to pay my January account at the Faculty Club and apply for lifetime free membership for my widow. This scheme had its snags, however, for the limbo in which I found myself was rather lonely, the only other person in the same situation being Lazarus. Theologians have complained for centuries how disappointingly uncommunicative he is, and I must confirm that he is not exactly a ball of fire. Besides, as Burns put it in *A Dream*, 'facts are chiels that winna ding an' downa be disputed'; despite all these dangers, I am alive, and unlike Lazarus I have lots to say.

My detractors in the audience that night asserted that I must have found the return journey a long climb. To this I could only reply with mention of one discovery I made in the nether regions. As Virgil escorted me through the Inferno, we came to one chamber of Hell in which there was thick, noxious smoke but little fire. Upon my enquiry, my guide replied, 'Och, that's the English — they're owre green tae burn!' Another Burns Supper was under way.

One can learn as much about a man from his attitude to the Devil as from his attitude to God, for the basic theology is the same. It is so basic that it is discussed by Scottish children from an early age. 'D'ye believe in the Devil, Tam?' a wee girlie asked her friend. 'Ach, no!' the laddie replied, 'It's just like Santa Claus; it's yer Faither.'

And it is taught thus in Scottish Schools of Theology, for New College cherishes the remark of the famous divine Charles Spurgeon advising his graduate students: 'When you speak of Heaven, let your face light up, let it be irradiated by a heavenly gleam, let your eye shine with reflected glory. But when you speak of Hell — your ordinary face will do.'

So the man in search of the real Robert Burns could do a lot worse than start in Hell, from which he addressed some of the poems, such as the *Address of Beelzebub*, headed thus in the manuscript: 'To the Right Honourable John, Earl of Breadalbane, President of the Right Honourable the Highland Society, which met, on the 23rd of May last, at the Shakespeare, Covent Garden, to concert ways and means to frustrate the designs of five hundred Highlanders who, as the Society were informed by Mr. McKenzie of Applecross, were so audacious as to attempt an escape from theire lawful lords and masters whose property they are by emigrating from the lands of Mr. McDonald of Glengary to the wilds of Canada, in search of that fantastic thing — LIBERTY' And the poem concludes:

> Go on, my lord! I lang to meet you
> An' in my house at hame to greet you;
> Wi' common lords ye shanna mingle,
> The benmost newk, beside the ingle
> At my right hand, assign'd your seat
> 'Tween Herod's hip, an' Polycrate;
> Or, if ye on your station tarrow,
> Between Almagro and Pizarro;
> A seat, I'm sure ye're weel deservin 't;
> An' till ye come — your humble servant
> BEELZEBUB.
> HELL, 1st June Anno Mundi 5790 (AD 1786)

From the very depths of Hell, Burns asserts the eternal value of *liberty*. Such writing is satire at its best, satire become a highly moral force encouraging society towards correct values and behaviour from Hell itself.

The Devil and Hell figure frequently in Burns poems. Consideration of Burns's attitudes to the Devil and Hell leads logically to consideration of Burns's treatment of the associated topics of drink and wenching, rounding out the picture of the Burns honoured at the annual Suppers; the Devil, the drink and the flesh proved the inspirations for some of his best writing.

The 17th- and 18th-century Calvinist view of Hell and the Devil was associated with the desire of the Scottish Church to dominate the moral lives of the people and to terrify them into Heaven rather than lead them there through sweetness and light. Black Russell in *The Holy Fair* is taken directly from life:

> His piercin words, like highlan swords,
>   Divide the joints an' marrow;
> His talk o' Hell, whare devils dwell,
>   Our vera 'Souls does harrow'
>   Wi' fright that day.

> A vast, unbottom'd, boundless Pit,
>   Filled fou o' lowan brunstane,
> Whase raging flame, an' scorching heat,
>   Wad melt the hardest whunstane!

This is the Miltonic Hell, Dante's vast purgatory, the Calvinist picture of roaring devils, furnaces for the eternal torment of the damned and everywhere the smell of brimstone. But Burns spearheads a revolution in thinking about the Devil and Hell by refusing to take the Calvinist picture seriously and by reducing the Devil to a homelier figure of fun, a melodramatic Devil set amidst the trappings of comic opera. The lines from *The Holy Fair* quoted above are followed immediately by lines which make clear Burns's satirical intent and which puncture the over-inflated impression just presented:

> The half-asleep start up wi' fear,
>   An' think they hear it roaran,
> When presently it does appear,
>   'Twas but some neebor snoran
>   Asleep that day.

An over-painted picture is also presented in *Holy Willie's Prayer:*

> When from my mother's womb I fell,
> Thou might hae plunged me deep in hell,
> To gnash my gooms, and weep, and wail,
>   In burning lakes,
> Where damned devils roar and yell
>   Chained to their stakes.

Detail from King's College, Cambridge

The damned devils of Willie's imagination have been so long in eternal torment weeping and wailing and gnashing their teeth that their teeth are completely worn away, leaving them to gnash their gums. The suspicion that Burns's tongue is in his cheek is confirmed by the satirical tone of the poem; this description of Hell is, after all, from the lips of Holy Willie. Similarly, Tam o' Shanter escapes from a Hell-fire too melodramatic to be taken seriously, as the simile makes clear:

> Ah, Tam! Ah, Tam! thou'll get thy fairin!
> In hell they'll roast thee like a herrin!

Burns's *Address to the Deil* makes clear at the very start that a homelier Devil than Milton's Satan is being addressed. Burns prefaces his poem with a couple of lines from *Paradise Lost*:

> O Prince, O chief of many throned pow'rs,
> That led th' embattl'd Seraphim to war.

Burns parallels these lines with his own apostrophe to a couthier Devil altogether:

> O thou, whatever title suit thee!
> Auld Hornie, Satan, Nick, or Clootie.

Compared to the malignant Miltonic Satan, Burns's Deil is greatly reduced in scale, permitting us to take a different attitude to 'Auld Hangie', 'Clootie', 'Auld Hornie', 'Auld Nick', 'Bob Mahoun'. The reduction in scale allows Burns to humanise his Deil. 'Hell, as our theologians paint it, particularly an eternal Hell, is a deeper damnation than I could bear to see the veriest scoundrel on earth plunged into' (to Miss Davies, April 6th, 1793). Burns carries this attitude so far that at the end of the *Address to the Deil* he wistfully suggests that even the Deil might conceivably repent enough to earn a chance of redemption:

> But fare you weel, auld Nickie-ben!
> O wad ye tak a thought an' men'!
> Ye aiblins might — I dinna ken —
>   Still hae a stake —
> I'm wae to think upo' yon den,
>   Ev'n for your sake.

Burns would have enjoyed a cartoon along exactly the same lines which appeared in *Punch* about twenty years ago. A rather bewildered Deil is shown wearing a halo and wandering bemused in Heaven while Gabriel says triumphantly to Raphael, 'And they said it couldn't be done!'

One must not mistake this humorous tone and think that Burns seeks to destroy the Devil altogether and drive him from people's minds. On the contrary, Burns wishes one to take a new attitude to a subtler Devil, the human temptation within rather than the sulphurous stage-figure without. The fourth stanza of the *Address to the Deil* introduces the subtler concept alongside the older picture of the raging Devil unroofing Christian churches:

> Whyles, ranging like a roaring lion,
> For prey, a' holes an' corners tryin;
> Whyles on the strong-wing'd Tempest flyin,
>   Tirlan the kirks;
> Whyles, in the human bosom pryin,
>   Unseen thou lurks.

And it is the subtler wiles of Auld Nick one sees at work on the poet
in his *Poem on Life* (addressed to Colonel de Peyster from Dumfries,
in 1796, the year of the poet's death):

> Ah! Nick, ah Nick it is na fair,
> First shewing us the tempting ware,
> Bright wines and bonnie lasses rare,
>   To put us daft;
> Syne weave, unseen, thy spider snare
>   O' hell's damned waft.
>
> Poor man the flie, aft bizzes bye,
> And aft as chance he comes thee nigh,
> Thy auld damned elbow yeuks wi' joy,
>   And hellish pleasure;
> Already in thy fancy's eye,
>   Thy sicker treasure.

It is this subtler devil who drives the hermit into the Wood of
Aberfeldy in *The Hermit*:

> No thought of guilt my bosom sours;
> Free-willed I fled from courtly bowers;
> For well I saw in halls and towers
>   That lust and pride,
> The arch-fiend's dearest, darkest powers,
>   In state preside.
>
> I saw mankind with vice incrusted;
> I saw that Honour's sword was rusted;
> That few for aught but folly lusted;
> That he was still deceived who trusted
>   To love or friend;
> And hither came, with men disgusted,
>   My life to end.[33]

It is difficult for the modern reader to sense truly the revolutionary daring of Burns's attitude to the Devil. Removed from the
oppressive atmosphere of the 'Auld Light' Calvinism that dominated
Burns's age, people no longer writhe on the penitent's stool while Black
Russell thunders about the eternal damnation of perpetual Hell-fire.

One no longer fears a physical Devil of great antiquity, whose very name 'Auld Nick' takes one back etymologically to the *niceras* of *Beowulf* a thousand years before Burns. And one no longer need fear reprisals for holding views of the Devil and moral behaviour contrary to those of severe Calvinist doctrine. In this regard, one often fails to appreciate fully the courage shown by Burns on the cutty stool at Mauchline, facing the degrading inquisitions and harsh penances of the Kirk as he paid the reckoning for his sins. Burns tells John Moore of the fate of *The Holy Fair* (Mauchline, August 2nd, 1787):

> I now began to be known in the neighbourhood as a maker of rhymes. The first of my poetic offspring that saw the light, was a burlesque lamentation on a quarrel between two reverend Calvinists, both of them *dramatis personae* in my *Holy Fair*. I had a notion myself, that the piece had some merit; but to prevent the worst, I gave a copy of it to a friend who was very fond of such things, and told him that I could not guess who was the author of it, but that I thought it pretty clever. With a certain description of the clergy, as well as laity, it met with a roar of applause. *Holy Willie's Prayer* next made its appearance, and alarmed the kirk-session so much, that they held several meetings to look over their spiritual artillery, if haply any of it might be pointed against profane rhymers. Unluckily for me, my wanderings led me on another side, within point-blank shot of their heaviest metal. This is the unfortunate story that gave rise to my printed poem, *The Lament*. This was a most melancholy affair, which I cannot yet bear to reflect on; and had very nearly given me one or two of the principal qualifications for a place among those who have lost the chart, and mistaken the reckoning of Rationality. I gave up my part of the farm to my brother; in truth it was only nominally mine; and made what little preparation was in my power for Jamaica.

These events in 1786 following Jean Armour's confession of pregnancy to the Kirk Session and Burns's chastising at their hands almost drove the poet to the point of madness and certainly led to his preparing for exile in Jamaica. Burns's laughing at the Devil is, therefore, laughing at the Auld Light Calvinists and running the serious and very real danger of their disapproval.

Burns's laughing at the Devil is also the laughter of saving grace, for only through laughter could the tears and madness be held in check. The Devil is still there, in the mind and in the heart, but the physical Devil is reduced to manageable human proportions at least. To this extent, Burns has rid Hell of some of its brunstane aspects; the poet of the plough also knew how to handle a harrow.

In Burns's laughter at the Devil is seen part of the reason for his being both universal in appeal and particularly Scottish. The universality of attraction subsists in his purging mankind of unreasoning fear of a physical Devil and the danger of ignoring the subtler temptations of Satan within the spirit. But the Devil who is mocked is of a marked Scottish nationality, playing bagpipes and indulging in reels and strathspeys and all sorts of high-jinks peculiar to Caledonia. This is not the Devil of the Calvinist Kirk so much as the Devil of mediaeval paintings and frescoes playing the bagpipes to torment the damned in Hell, the Devil to whom is likened Chaucer's gargoyle Miller driving the pilgrims from London in haste along the road to Canterbury in the General Prologue to *Canterbury Tales*, his cavernous grin like Hell-mouth of the miracle and mystery plays. Burns did not learn of this Devil from the Kirk but at his nurse's knee, as he tells Moore:

> In my infant and boyish days, too, I owed much to an old woman who resided in the family, remarkable for her ignorance, credulity and superstition. She had, I suppose, the largest collection in the country of tales and songs concerning devils, ghosts, fairies, brownies, witches, warlocks, spunkies, kelpies, elf-candles, dead-lights, wraiths, apparitions, cantraips, giants, enchanted towers, dragons, and other trumpery. This cultivated the latent seeds of poetry. . . .

This is the sort of Devil found in Burns's undated letter to Captain Francis Grose in which the poet tells three superstitious tales about the old church at Alloway, already a ruin in his time. Gilbert Burns records that when Grose came to stay at Carse House, the home of Robert's friend Captain Robert Riddel of Glenriddel, the poet and the antiquary were 'unco pack and thick thegither.' Burns requested that Grose make a drawing of Alloway Kirk, and the antiquary agreed on condition that Burns supply a witch-story to accompany it upon publication. This was the genesis of Burns's prose account to Grose, and, of course, of *Tam o' Shanter*, later published in Grose's *Antiquities of Scotland*.

There is no need, I am sure, to go to great lengths to demonstrate that *Tam o' Shanter* is Burns's and Scotland's comic masterpiece, for in this I should merely be stating the obvious. Suffice it to recall that Tam is the archetypal social drinker who feels that 'Time, gentlemen, please' are the most unpleasant words in any language. Floating home from the pub on his horse one dark and stormy night, he comes upon a witches' orgy in Alloway's auld haunted kirk and observes that the coven are being led in their celebration of their Black Mass by the comic Devil playing the bagpipes.

> And, Vow! Tam saw an unco sight!
> Warlocks and witches in a dance;
> Nae cotillion brent new frae France,
> But hornpipes, jigs, strathspeys, and reels,
> Put life and mettle in their heels.
> A winnock-bunker in the east,
> There sat auld Nick, in shape o' beast;
> A towzie tyke, black, grim, and large,
> To gie them music was his charge:
> He screw'd the pipes and gart them skirl,
> Till roof and rafters a' did dirl.

The narrator points out quite reasonably that witches are as a rule old hags:

> But wither'd beldams, auld and droll,
> Rigwoodie hags wad spean a foal,
> Lowping and flinging on a crummock,
> I wonder didna turn thy stomach.

But Tam is so filled with drink and lust that he shares the Devil's taste in witches. Tam and Satan are both very taken with one young witch in the coven who is wearing a mini-underskirt made for her by a very Scottish grandmother who economised on material, much to Tam's delight. As Nannie kicks her legs higher and higher into the air, Tam sees a vision scarcely Heavenly at which he cannot resist calling out:

> But here my Muse her wing maun cour;
> Sic flights are far beyond her pow'r:
> To sing how Nannie lap and flang,
> (A souple jade she was, and strang),
> And how Tam stood, like ane bewitch'd,
> And thought his very een enrich'd;
> Even Satan glowr'd, and fidg'd fu' fain,
> And hotch'd and blew wi' might and main;
> Till first ae caper, syne anither,
> Tam tint his reason a' thegither,
> And roars out, 'Weel done, Cutty-sark!'
> And in an instant all was dark:
> And scarcely had he Maggie rallied,
> When out the hellish legion sallied.

Readers will recall that a tea clipper on the China run which was the fastest of its class was named the *Cutty Sark* after this incident,[34] and that a well-known brand of Scotch whisky which must remain nameless commemorates both the ship and the poem on its label. During these animadversions, I have left Tam being hotly pursued by the Hellish legion, which is headed by the strapping wench in the economical clothing. Tam in his panic recalls that evil spirits cannot follow a victim over running water (which stands presumably for Christian baptism) and charges for the Brig o' Doon:

> For Nannie, far before the rest,
> Hard upon noble Maggie prest,
> And flew at Tam wi' furious ettle;
> But little wist she Maggie's mettle —
> Ae spring brought off her master hale,
> But left behind her ain gray tail:
> The carlin claught her by the rump,
> And left poor Maggie scarce a stump.

When the obvious and famous moral is pointed, one has not finished with either Captain Grose or Burns's comic Devil. The two appear again in humorous juxtaposition in the short poem *On Captain Francis Grose*:

> The Devil got notice that Grose was a-dying,
> So whip! at the summons, old Satan came flying;
> But when he approach'd where poor Francis lay moaning,
> And saw each bed-post with its burden a-groaning,
> Astonished! confounded! cry'd Satan, by God,
> I'll want 'im, ere I take such a damnable load.

In the same joking vein is the final stanza of Burns's *Epitaph on Holy Willie*, in which his 'brunstane devilship' is warned that having Willie in the nether regions can redound only to Satan's discredit:

> But hear me, Sir, de'il as ye are,
> Look something to your credit;
> A coof like him wou'd stain your name,
> If it were kent ye did it.

This is the Devil whose hellish torments are equated by Burns with toothache in *Address to the Toothache*:

> Whare'er that place be, priests ca' hell,
> Whare a' the tones o' mis'ry yell,
> An' plagues in ranked number tell,
>   In deadly raw,
> Thou, Tooth-ache, surely bear'st the bell
>   Aboon them a'!

> O! thou grim mischief-makin chiel,
> That gars the notes o' discord squeel,
> Till human-kind aft dance a reel
>   In gore a shoe thick,
> Gie a' the faes o' Scotland's weal
>   A Towmond's Tooth-Ache!

And this is the Devil whom one pities as he is tormented by a nagging wife. Burns's version of the international *Devil and Kate* story is to be found in his reworking of an ancient ballad, *The Carle of Kellyburn Braes*:

> Then Satan has travell'd again wi' his pack,
>   Hey and the rue grows bonie wi' thyme;
> And to her auld husband he's carried her back,
>   And the thyme it is wither'd and rue is in prime.

> I hae been a devil the feck o' my life,
>   Hey and the rue grows bonie wi' thyme;
> But ne'er was in hell till I met wi' a wife,
>   And the thyme it is wither'd and rue is in prime.

The Devil has his uses, of course — he is good at carrying off excisemen. This is mentioned in *Scotch Drink*:

> Thae curst horse-leeches o' th' Excise,
> Wha mak the Whisky stills their prize!
> Haud up thy han' Deil! ance, twice, thrice!
>   There, sieze the blinkers!
> An' bake them up in brunstane pies
>   For poor damn'd Drinkers.

And this is stressed with glee in *The Deil's Awa'* with its chorus of universal rejoicing:

> The deil's awa the deil's awa
> The deil's awa wi' th' Exciseman.
> He's danc'd awa he's danc'd awa
> He's danc'd awa wi' th' Exciseman.

Such a Devil is useful, too, for the Jacobites in *Come, Boat Me O'er To Charlie*:

> But O, to see auld Nick gaun hame,
> And Charlie's faes before him!

This comic Devil is peculiarly Scottish in his behaviour. Only of Scotland could *Tam o' Shanter* be written, for only in Scotland is the Devil a sensual figure of delighted fun at the same time as a real source of temptation in the mind of man. Burns the national poet has caught perfectly the Scottish attitude to Hell and the Devil of popular jokes, such as the one about the minister with six sons, all of whom become ministers in their turn, save for one scapegrace. One Christmas, the black sheep came home unexpectedly, to find his father and brothers warming themselves by the hearth. He claimed their attention by relating to them a dream about Hell he had had the previous night. 'What was it like?' asked the ministers, their professional interest aroused. 'Oh,' said the black sheep, 'It was jist the same as here — I couldna get near the fire fer meenisters.'

A hot gospeller was monotonously relating his itinerary. 'Last month, brethren, I was fighting the Devil in Wick. A fortnight ago, I was fighting him in Inverness. Last week, I fought him in Dundee. On Tuesday, I fought him in Falkirk. To-night, brethren, I am fighting him in Haddington.' The inebriated voice of Jock Hirsel, A stentorian shepherd from the Lammermoor, broke in. 'That's richt, man. Keep haudin' the b. . . Sooth.'[35]

At the ordination of one of the Auld Light Calvinist preachers, Burns has the comic Devil stoking the fires in his ovens in preparation for doing battle with his new opponent, M'Kinlay of Kilmarnock:

> Auld Hornie did the Laigh Kirk watch,
>   Just like a winkin baudrons:
> And ay he catch'd the tither wretch,
>   To fry them in his caudrons;
> But now his Honor maun detach,
>   Wi' a' his brimstone squadrons,
>   Fast, fast this day.

Yet the laughter merely keeps at bay the tears and the pain of Calvinist condemnation. Burns has to endure the Kirk's censure of his affair with a Dumfries blonde of assailable virtue, Anna Park, a barmaid at the Globe Inn by whom Burns had a child. The poet maintains his defiance in *The Gowden Locks of Anna*:

> Yestreen I had a pint o' wine,
> A place where body saw na;
> Yestreen lay on this breast o' mine
> The gowden locks of Anna. . . .
>
> The kirk and state may join and tell;
> To do sic things I manna:
> The kirk and state may gae to hell,
> And I shall gae to Anna.
> She is the sunshine o' my e'e,
> To live but her I canna:
> Had I on earth but wishes three,
> The first should be my Anna.

The real Devil, in leading Burns astray with women and drink, reduces the poet's self-esteem and his ability to write poetry. Burns complains unhappily in his poem *To William Stewart*:

> Satan, I fear thy sooty claws,
> I hate thy brunstane stink,
> And ay I curse the luckless cause,
> The wicked soup o' drink.
>
> In vain I would forget my woes
> In idle rhyming clink,
> For past redemption damn'd in Prose
> I can do nought but drink.

And eventually the real Devil has his way with Burns. On his deathbed, he wrote the following *Lines to John Rankin* which did not reach Adamhill until after the poet's passing:

> He who of Rankin sang, lies stiff and dead,
> And a green grassy hillock hides his head;
> Alas! Alas! a devilish change indeed.

The tears are not far below the surface of the laughter of love, and that is what gives the laughter its poignancy.

8

Leeze me on Drink!

John Barleycorn was a hero bold,
  Of noble enterprise,
For if you do but taste his blood,
  'Twill make your courage rise.

'Twill make a man forget his woe;
  'Twill heighten all his joy:
'Twill make the widow's heart to sing,
  Tho' the tear were in her eye.

Then let us toast John Barleycorn,
  Each man a glass in hand;
And may his great posterity
  Ne'er fail in old Scotland!

To pass from discussion of Burns and the Devil to consideration of Burns and the drink or of Burns and the flesh is not really to change the subject, for Auld Nick gave Burns his taste for two of the finer things in life — whisky and women. Those who attend Burns Suppers in search of St Robert are more likely to be disappointed than those who seek Rab Mossgiel the drinker and wencher, for one cannot deny the legend its basis in truths to be found in the biography.

The poet's detractors take the extreme view of Burns's drinking first articulated by James Currie:

> Hitherto Burns, though addicted to excess in social parties, had abstained from the habitual use of strong liquors, and his constitution had not suffered any permanent injury from the irregularities of his conduct. In Dumfries, temptations to *the sin that so easily beset him*, continually presented themselves; and his irregularities grew by degrees into habits. These temptations unhappily occurred during his engagements in the business of his office, as well as during his hours of relaxation; and though he clearly foresaw the consequence of yielding to them, his appetites and sensations, which could not pervert the dictates of his judgment, finally triumphed over the powers of his will.

There can be little doubt that by modern standards Burns was what one would classify clearly as an alcoholic. Were he to walk today into a meeting of Alcoholics Anonymous, he would be greeted with open arms as a supreme challenge, and modern-day psychologists would strive valiantly to effect his cure; either process would, if successful, rob the world of some great poetry, of course.

Burns's gallant defenders on this point would assert that one errs in judging Burns's drinking by modern standards and demand that he be judged in the context of his age. In his time, some gentlemen held it a singular point of honour to be drunken even before breakfast-time, and records have been kept of the almost unbelievable amounts of claret and whisky consumed by Boswell and his friends. Perhaps in comparison to such men Burns would appear slightly stuffy, though I personally doubt it. At any rate, the biography is against the disclaimer made by Gilbert Burns in a letter to Mrs. Dunlop:

> Yet, notwithstanding . . . the praise he has bestowed on Scotch drink, (which seems to have misled his historians,) I do not recollect, during these seven years, nor till towards the end of his commencing author, (when his growing celebrity occasioned his being often in company) to have ever seen him intoxicated; nor was he at all given to drinking.

I certainly think the poet's widow rather pious when she stated that neither before nor after their marriage did she see the poet intoxicated, unable to make his way home or incapable upon his arrival there; she never saw the poet the worse for drink. Maybe so, but there must have been occasions on which she saw him the *better* for drink. It is, after all, no teetotaller who gives this fine picture of alcoholic conviviality involving William Nicol, Allan Masterton and the poet one night in Moffat:

> O Willie brew'd a peck o' maut,
>   And Rob and Allan cam to see;
> Three blyther hearts, that lee lang night,
>   Ye wad na found in Christendie. . .
>
> Wha first shall rise to gang awa,
>   A cuckold, coward loun is he!
> Wha first beside his chair shall fa',
>   He is the king amang us three!

> We are na fou, we're nae that fou,
> But just a drappie in our e'e;
> The cock may craw, the day may daw,
> And ay we'll taste the barley bree.

And it is no sufferer from only an occasional hangover who gives the following warning in *Drinking*:

> My bottle is a holy pool,
> That heals the wounds o' care an' dool;
> And pleasure is a wanton trout,
> An ye drink it, ye'll find him out.

Similar to this is the picture in the *Address to the Deil* of the over-imbiber falling easy victim to the lure of the Devil-sent Wills-o'-the-Wisp:

> An' aft your moss-traversing Spunkies
> Decoy the wight that late an' drunk is:
> The bleezan, curst, mischievous monkies
> Delude his eyes,
> Till in some miry slough he sunk is,
> Ne'er mair to rise.

Lest there be any doubt that Burns was a man of expert and most intimate knowledge of whisky, the poet has left a verse sermon on his favourite Biblical text, Proverbs 31.6-7. In the contemporary Scottish psalter the text ran as follows:

> Gie him strong Drink until he wink,
> That's sinking in despair;
> An' liquor guid, to fire his bluid,
> That's prest wi' grief an' care:
> There let him bowse an' deep carouse,
> Wi' bumpers flowing o'er,
> Till he forgets his loves or debts,
> An' minds his griefs no more.

Burns explicates this text with fine perception and moving eloquence, demonstrating to all the depth of Solomon's wisdom and his own insightful reading of the words 'strong drink' as *Scotch Drink*:

> Let other Poets raise a fracas
> 'Bout vines, an' wines, an' druken Bacchus,
> An' crabbed names an' stories wrack us,
>   An' grate our lug,
> I sing the juice Scotch bear can mak us,
>   In glass or jug.
>
> O thou, my Muse! guid, auld Scotch Drink!
> Whether thro' wimplin worms thou jink,
> Or, richly brown, ream owre the brink,
>   In glorious faem,
> Inspire me, till I lisp an' wink,
>   To sing thy name!

It is significant that in order to present his interpretation of Holy Writ Burns makes for his congregation the ultimate sacrifice in that he deserts Coila for another Muse, whisky itself. That the sacrifice is worth his while is amply borne out by the powerful peroration to his sermon:

> Fortune, if thou'll but gie me still
> Hale breeks, a scone, an' Whisky gill,
> An' rowth o' rhyme to rave at will,
>   Tak a' the rest,
> An' deal 't about as thy blind skill
>   Directs thee best.

Examination of Burns's poetry reveals four main motives for the poet's passing of some of Scotland's finest product over his tonsils. The first motive is the most obvious one, that of being sociable. In the warmth of alcoholic conviviality in a public house, one can find, at least temporarily, a simulacrum of happiness in which acquaintances can appear as friends and emotions can seem genuine. In Poosie Nancy's pub in Mauchline with the jolly beggars or in Kirkton Jean's in Kirkoswald with Tam o' Shanter and Souter Johnie might be found escape into an albeit spurious state of society in which all Burns's ideals of pride, dignity, independence of mind and the laughter of love might be realised, for the moment:

> But pleasures are like poppies spread,
> You seize the flower, its bloom is shed;
> Or like the snow falls in the river,

A moment white — then melts for ever;
Or like the borealis race,
That flit ere you can point their place;
Or like the rainbow's lovely form
Evanishing amid the storm.

Such is the temporary nature of the ale-house's vision of the ideal
world, as Burns realised full well, but the alcoholic vision of happiness
was of vital importance to him in his artistic motivations, spurring
him in compensation to write poetry which would in a more lasting
way enshrine his ideals in firmer stuff; *exegi monumentum aere perennius*.

The alcoholic conviviality of the public house is immortalised in
Tam o' Shanter, the poem which has put the little Ayrshire village of
Kirkoswald on the literary map. The poet's mother, Agnes Brown,
was born in the parish, at Craigenton Farm, in 1732, to Gilbert Brown
and Agnes Rennie. A brother named Samuel Brown lived in Ballochneil Farm, just to the south-west, and it was there that Burns
boarded with his uncle in 1776 when the seventeen-year-old poet forsook sines and cosines for the curves of Peggy Thomson. In his history
of Kirkoswald Parish, the present incumbent, James Guthrie, offers
an account of the genesis of *Tam o' Shanter* at variance with the tale
of Burns's collaboration with Francis Grose afforded by Gilbert Burns.
Rev. Guthrie gives the local details with great charm:

> Burns's uncle, Samuel Brown, had a bosom friend in his near
> neighbour Douglas Graham, of Laigh Park. Graham also worked
> the shore farm of Shanter and had there in the bay a boat called
> 'Tam'. It was because of this that he became know to the locals as
> 'Tam o' Shanter' . . . Tam o' Shanter, as we will now call him, as
> well as farming, brewed ale at his Park Farm, and here, with his
> neighbour from Ballochneil, no doubt they would spend many an
> evening mixing and tasting the home brew! Once a week Tam
> would take his brew to the town of Ayr, often accompanied by a
> neighbour of his Shanter farm, one John Davidson, a Souter
> (shoemaker) from Glenfoot, immortalised by Burns as 'Souter
> Johnie'. The inspiration for that great poem came from one of
> these trips to the County Town.
>
> The story is told that Burns and a school friend, John Niven, set
> out one day from Shanter Bay to spend a day on Ailsa Craig. Not
> long after they left, a storm got up and they had to turn back.
> Having tied-up, they took shelter at Shanter farm, where the
> farmer's wife was waiting for the return of her husband from

market. She was a Helen McTaggart, of Hogston, about half a mile along the Shore, and was greatly given to superstition; and so her anger for the lateness of her husband, mixed with the fear she had for the storm, manifested itself with a great outpouring of curses and prophesying . . . As it happened, the same storm that inconvenienced Burns inconvenienced Tam; for coming over Brown Carrick, a hill near Maybole, he lost his good blue bonnet in which he kept his money. On arriving at Shanter, all Hell was let loose! The next morning at Ballochneil, young Robert appeared with a rough draft of his famous poem, which he completed later in life. Of the validity of this story no one can tell, but of the plot and the characters there is no doubt that they are all based in the times and the folk-lore of the people of Kirkoswald Parish in the 1770s.[36]

It is, of course, not impossible to reconcile this account with that of Gilbert Burns and to assume that Burns added to these Kirkoswald goings-on those of Alloway Kirk to make the foundation of his poem. If, indeed, the poem had its genesis in Kirkoswald in the 1770s but was not published until April of 1791, this would explain the writing of the poem under the influence of Coila so often remarked by those who note that Burns's later period was mainly under the influence of a lesser Muse.

The story of the poem is very Scottish in its setting, its plot, its characters, its action, its moral and, above all, its humour, but Burns has also been able to transcend merely local interest to make his poem of universal relevance in its picture of the spurious Heaven of the public house which so fatally attracts the poet:

> Ae market-night,
> Tam had got planted unco right;
> Fast by an ingle, bleezing finely,
> Wi' reaming swats, that drank divinely;
> And at his elbow, Souter Johnie,
> His ancient, trusty, drouthy crony;
> Tam lo'ed him like a vera brither;
> They had been fou for weeks thegither.
> The night drave on wi' sangs and clatter;
> And ay the ale was growing better:
> The landlady and Tam grew gracious,
> Wi' favours, secret, sweet, and precious:
> The Souter tauld his queerest stories;
> The landlord's laugh was ready chorus:

The storm without might rair and rustle,
Tam did na mind the storm a whistle.

Care, mad to see a man sae happy,
E'en drown'd himsel amang the nappy:
As bees flee hame wi' lades o' treasure,
The minutes wing'd their way wi' pleasure:
Kings may be blest, but Tam was glorious,
O'er a' the ills o' life victorious!

Tam O' Shanter Statue, Kirkoswald

This is scarcely moderation in the true Aristotelian sense; it is, rather, moderation along the lines of the old Scotsman MacThusalah who, when asked the secret of his longevity, replied, 'Moderation in all things; I take a little water with my whisky and a lot of whisky with my water.' But behind the picture of intoxicated mirth and pseudo-happiness there lie the ideals being violated, not the ideals so much of stern Calvinism as those important to Burns — dignity, independence, strength of character.

The second motive for regular imbibing is to keep oneself happy in one's own company as much as in a social setting, and to gain thereby further supposed realisation of one's ideals. Here, for instance, is the *apolgia* offered in *The Holy Fair*:

> Leeze me on Drink! it gies us mair
> Than either School or Colledge:
> It kindles Wit, it waukens Lear,
> It pangs us fou o' Knowledge.
> Be 't whisky-gill or penny-wheep,
> Or onie stronger potion,
> It never fails, on drinkin deep,
> To kittle up our notion,
> By night or day.

The postscript to *The Author's Earnest Cry and Prayer to the Scotch Representatives in the House of Commons* climaxes in the association of whisky and the poet's most highly valued ideal — freedom:

> Sages their solemn een may steek,
> An' raise a philosophic reek,
> An' physically causes seek,
> In clime an' season,
> But tell me Whisky's name in Greek,
> I'll tell the reason.
>
> Scotland, my auld, respected Mither!
> Tho' whyles ye moistify your leather,
> Till when ye speak, ye aiblins blether;
> Yet deil-mak-matter!
> Freedom and Whisky gang thegither,
> Tak aff your whitter.

Again, behind the levity lies the same serious point — the apparent happiness brought by drink is spurious. Whatever the temporary happiness ale brings, the price in human dignity is high:

> O gude ale comes and gude ale goes,
> Gude ale gars me sell my hose,
> Sell my hose and pawn my shoon,
> Gude ale keeps my heart aboon.

In vino veritas. Drink seems to keep the heart aboon, but scan the price. And when the heart is not aboon, when the heart is breaking, the tears are near the surface of the laughter once again, as in *Scotch Drink's* more serious moments:

> Thou clears the head o' doited Lear;
> Thou chears the heart o' dropping Care;
> Thou strings the nerves o' Labor-sair,
>   At's weary toil;
> Thou ev'n brightens dark Despair,
>   Wi' gloomy smile.

It is with little enthusiasm that one raises a couple of cheers for gloomy smile.

The third motive for drinking is that it leads to lust, another sensual snare in the path of human frailty. One prime example of the juxtaposition of drinking and lust is, of course, to be found in *Tam o' Shanter*, in the scene of Tam's observing the dance of the one cutty sark as performed by Nannie. That Burns did not find models in only Kirkoswald pubs is demonstrated in *The Jolly Beggars: A Cantata*, for which the inspiration resulted from a visit with John Richmond and John Smith to the public house run by Mrs. Gibson ('Poosie Nancy') in Mauchline. The merry vagrants in their cups gave Burns the impetus to write his Golliard cantata of which the following is an extract portraying the association of drink and lust:

> The Caird prevail'd — th' unblushing fair
>   In his embraces sunk;
> Partly wi' Love o'ercome sae sair,
>   An' partly she was drunk:
> Sir Violino with an air,
>   That show'd a man o' spunk,
> Wish'd unison between the pair,
>   An' made the bottle clunk
>   To their health that night

But hurchin Cupid shot a shaft,
   That play'd a Dame a shavie —
The Fiddler rak'd her, fore and aft,
   Behint the Chicken cavie:
Her lord, a wight of Homer's craft,
   Tho' limpan wi' the Spavie,
He hirpl'd up an' lap like daft,
   An' shor'd them Dainty Davie
            O' boot that night.

He was a care-defying blade,
   As ever Bacchus listed!
Tho' fortune sair upon him laid,
   His heart she ever miss'd it.
He had no wish but — to be glad,
   Nor want but — when he thristed;
He hated nought but — to be sad,
   An' thus the Muse suggested
            His sang that night.

This leads one to the final motive for Burns's drinking, to find in John Barleycorn inspiration for verse. The association of drinking

Poosie Nansie's, Mauchline

and rhyming is made clear in the *Second Epistle to Davie*, an epistle prefixed to the poems of David Sillar upon their publication in Kilmarnock in 1789. Burns tells Davie rather wistfully:

> For me, I'm on Parnassus brink,
> Rivan the words tae gar them clink;
> Whyles daez't wi' love, whyles daez't wi' drink,
> Wi' jads or masons;
> An' whyles, but ay owre late, I think
> Braw sober lessons.

While noting that love is an inspiration, one sees immediately alongside it the drink and the wry reflection of the last line of the stanza.

The same wry note enters the first line of the following stanza from Burns's *Epistle to William Creech*, in the form of an obituary for the Edinburgh publisher:

> Poor Burns — even Scotch Drink canna quicken,
> He cheeps like some bewilder'd chicken,
> Scar'd frae its minnie and the cleckin
> By hoodie-craw:
> Brief's gien his heart an unco kickin,
> Willie's awa.

The ultimate confession of the poet's reliance on drink as inspiration comes in *Scotch Drink* when for a moment confessional intrudes upon the sermon:

> O Whisky! soul o' plays an' pranks!
> Accept a Bardie's gratefu' thanks!
> When wanting thee, what tuneless cranks
> Are my poor Verses!
> Thou comes — they rattle i' their ranks
> At ither's arses!

Alas, Burns mentions his reliance on drink too often and in too varied contexts for the apologist's comfort. Drinking brought the poet social warmth, private solace, sexual opportunity and poetic inspiration, and for the last of these one must in gratitude forgive the other three. Drinking obviously met some deep need in the poet's psyche, leading him to fall so short of his ideals that he was inspired to give his ideals their finest expression in consequence. This is not paradox-

ical, for the self-perpetuating cycle of rise and fall to rise again is
psychologically valid. In personal terms, however, there is something
upsetting about the deep need for drink in the poet whose memory
one seeks to honour. When Burns spells out his four motives for drinking to fellow-poets, there is pain behind the laughter and sadness brings
the tear to the eye when the train of thought reaches its climax thus
in the *Epistle to J. Lapraik* and the *Epistle to John Goldie*:

> But Mauchline Race or Mauchline Fair,
> I should be proud to meet you there;
> We'se gie ae night's discharge to care,
>   If we forgather,
> An' hae a swap o' rhymin-ware,
>   Wi' ane anither.

> The four-gill chap, we'se gar him clatter,
> An' kirs'n him wi' reekin water;
> Syne we'll sit down an' tak our whitter,
>   To chear our heart;
> An' faith, we'se be acquainted better
>   Before we part. . . .

> There's naething like the honest nappy;
> Whare'll ye e'er see men sae happy,
> Or women sonsie, saft and sappy,
>   'Tween morn and morn,
> As them wha like to taste the drappie
>   In glass or horn.

> I've seen me daez't upon a time,
> I scarce could wink or see a styme;
> Just ae hauf-mutchkin does me prime,
>   (Ought less, is little)
> Then back I rattle on the rhyme,
>   As gleg's a whittle.

If one can find in Burns's treatment of the topic of drink part of
the laughter of love that is at once so Scottish in expression and so
universal in appreciation, one also finds pain behind the pleasure and
is forced to admit that there is something pathetic as well as much
that is grand in the Muse Coila who has to approach her bard with a
bottle concealed in the folds of her garment.

9
Confess I must — At times I'm fash'd wi' fleshly lust

But sure as three times three mak nine,
I see by ilka score and line,
This chap will dearly like our kin',
So leeze me on thee, Robin.

Guid faith quo' scho I doubt you Stir,
Ye'll gar the lasses lie aspar;
But twenty fauts ye may hae waur —
So blessins on thee, Robin.

Robin was a rovin' boy,
Rantin' rovin', rantin' rovin';
Robin was a rovin' boy,
Rantin' rovin' Robin.

No-one familiar with Burns's biography can entertain any doubts about Burns's expertise with the ladies as well as with whisky. When the lasses lay aspar, Burns was not one to hesitate. He would certainly never have run into the trouble that confronted one innocent Scottish youth on his first visit to London. Wandering into Soho, the youth was accosted by a coloured girl who said to him, 'Would you like to come home with me, dearie?' To which the youth replied, 'What on earth would I do in Africa?'

It is a matter of record in the poems and the letters that Burns enjoyed a nice piece of houghmagandie and was not afraid to say so. In his autobiographical letter he tells John Moore (Mauchline, August 2nd, 1787):

But, far beyond all other impulses of my heart, was *un penchant a l'adorable moitié du genre humain*. My heart was completely tinder, and was eternally lighted up by some goddess or other; and, as in every other warfare in this world my fortune was various, sometimes I was received with favour and sometimes I was mortified with a repulse.

107

In the *Epistle to J. Lapraik*, Burns confesses as follows to that old Scottish bard:

> There's ae wee faut they whiles lay to me,
> I like the lasses — Gude forgie me!
> For monie a Plack they wheedle frae me,
>   At dance or fair:
> May be some ither thing they gie me
>   They weel can spare.

The first note struck is therefore one of laughter and light-hearted fun. Burns sees sins far worse than houghmagandie, and consequently enjoys freedom of expression on the pleasant topic of physical relations between the sexes. Burns's bawdry may be found in plenty in *The Merry Muses of Caledonia*, but it will suffice here to quote from some of the verse suppressed from the Kilmarnock Edition. Here, for instance, is the shameless song from *The Jolly Beggars: A Cantata* on the lips of a lady whose values are not exactly those of conventional respectability. 'I once was a maid, though I cannot tell when,' she begins, then traces her autobiography from a certain limited perspective:

> The first of my Loves was a swaggering blade,
> To rattle the thundering drum was his trade;
> His leg was so tight and his cheek was so ruddy,
> Transported I was with my Sodger Laddie.
>
> But the godly old Chaplain left him in the lurch,
> The sword I forsook for the sake of the church;
> He ventured the Soul, and I risked the Body
> 'Twas then I prov'd false to my Sodger Laddie.
>
> Full soon I grew sick of my sanctified Sot,
> The Regiment at large for a husband I got;
> From the gilded Spontoon to the Fife I was ready,
> I asked no more but a Sodger Laddie.

In similar vein are such songs as *The Taylor, The Lass That Made The Bed To Me* (which Burns says 'was composed on an amour of Charles II., when skulking in the North, about Aberdeen, in the time of the Usurpation') *O Steer Her Up and Hand Her Gaun,* and the bard's song from *The Jolly Beggars: A Cantata* — 'I am a Bard of no regard':

> Their tricks an' craft hae put me daft,
>   They've ta'en me in, an' a' that,
> But clear your decks an' here 's the sex!
>   I like the jads for a' that.

Gentler and less shameless are verses seeing such matters from the girl's point of view, such as *Ye Hae Lien Wrang, Lassie,* the warnings about vile seducers in stanza 10 of *The Cotter's Saturday Night,* and *The Ruined Maid's Lament.* In a letter to William Dunbar, Burns notes wryly (Ellisland, January 14th, 1790):

> To a Father who himself knows the world, the thought that he shall have Sons to usher into it, must fill him with dread; but if he have Daughters, the prospect in a thoughtful moment is apt to shock him.

Many of the humorous poems about sexual conquest are autobiographical, and show Burns striking another pose to set beside the ploughman and patriotic poses, that of the stallion in high demand. In *Halloween,* for instance, Nell is led astray by Rab:

> The lasses staw frae 'mang them a',
>   To pou their stalks o' corn;
> But Rab slips out, an' jinks about,
>   Behint the muckle thorn:
> He grippet Nelly hard an' fast;
>   Loud skirl'd a' the lasses
> But her tap-pickle maist was lost,
>   When kiutlin in the Fause-house
>   Wi' him that night.

The Tarbolton Lasses surveys the girls of that neighbourhood and contains information to their disadvantage gleaned from the young poet's experiences, while *Mauchline Belles* performs the same service for Mauchline in such a charming expression of *hubris* that it merits quotation in full:

> O leave novels, ye Mauchline belles.
>   Ye're safer at your spinning wheel;
> Such witching books, are baited hooks
>   For rakish rooks like Rob Mossgiel.
> Your fine Tom Jones and Grandisons

> They make your youthful fancies reel;
> They heat your brains, and fire your veins,
> And then you're prey for Rob Mossgiel.
>
> Beware a tongue that's smoothly hung;
> A heart that warmly seems to feel;
> That feelin heart but acts a part,
> 'Tis rakish art in Rob Mossgiel.
> The frank address, the soft caress,
> Are worse than poisoned darts of steel;
> The frank address, and politesse,
> Are all finesse in Rob Mossgiel.

This comic Devil is a paper tiger who can be avoided by not reading Fielding or Richardson, though the twinkle in the eye plays havoc of its own, no doubt. The twinkle is certainly shamelessly in evidence when Burns meets his Muse in *The Vision*, a Muse who reveals more leg than is normally thought seemly on Parnassus:

> Down flow'd her robe, a tartan sheen,
> Till half a leg was scrimply seen;
> And such a leg! my bonie Jean
>   Could only peer it;
> Sae straught, sae taper, tight and clean,
>   Nane else came near it.

Poor Coila has to put up with much her Classical sisters did not experience. Where other poets are reticent about the sexual attraction of the Muses they serve, this is the first thing to come to Burns's mind.

In some other poems and letters, however, notes more defiant, cynical and pornographic are struck, to the discomfort at least of apologists in search of St Robert. Also suppressed from the Kilmarnock Edition was *The Fornicator*, a song enshrining the poet's affair in 1785 with Elizabeth Paton. In one stanza, the irrepressible poet in church bows his head in contrition, only to see in the process his girl-friend's legs and become excited all over again:

> Before the Congregation wide
> I pass'd the muster fairly,
> My handsome Betsey by my side,
> We gat our ditty rarely;

> But my downcast eye by chance did spy
> What made my lips to water,
> Those limbs so clean where I, between,
> Commenc'd a Fornicator.

The Poet's Welcome to his Illegitimate Child contains the following defiant stanza throwing the poet's philandering in the teeth of his severest critics:

> Tho' now they ca' me, Fornicator,
> And tease my name in kintra clatter,
> The mair they talk, I'm kend the better;
>   E'en let them clash!
> An auld wife's tongue's a feckless matter
>   To gie ane fash.

I should class as pornographic portions of Burns's letter to John Arnot, recounting the poet's sexual conquest of Jean Armour (April, 1786):

> My mouth watered deliciously, to see a young fellow, after a few idle, common-place stories from a gentleman in black, strip & go to bed with a young girl, & no one durst say, black was his eye; while I, for just doing the same thing, only wanting that ceremony, am made a Sunday's laughing-stock, & abused like a pick-pocket.

Burns lived in a moral climate vastly different from the modern one in sexual matters, but while one sympathises with the predicament he articulates in this letter there can be little doubt that what follows would be considered pornographic an any age. In similar vein is Burns's letter to Robert Ainslie (Mauchline, March 3rd, 1788), describing the good ploughing the poet gave Jean Armour upon his being reunited with her. And there is a depth of experience behind the advice given to his brother William Burns (Ellisland, February 10th, 1790):

> Whoring is a most ruinous expensive species of dissipation; is spending a poor fellow's money with which he ought to clothe & support himself nothing? Whoring has ninety nine chances in a hundred to bring on a man the most nauseous & excrutiating diseases to which Human nature is liable; are disease & an impaired constitution trifling considerations? All this independent of the criminality of it.

Of a similar, though less explicit nature is the warning contained in the *Epistle to a Young Friend* addressed to Andrew Aiken:

> The sacred lowe o' weel plac'd love,
> Luxuriantly indulge it;
> But never tempt th' illicit rove,
> Tho' naething should divulge it:
> I wave the quantum o' the sin;
> The hazard of concealing:
> But Och! it hardens a' within,
> And petrifies the feeling!

There is a refreshing frankness to Burns's carnal enjoyment which defies the best efforts of bowdlerizing editors and tends to disarm the strict moralist of the right to judge and condemn. But behind the sheer humour of some poems and the frank carnality of others may be discerned a third and totally different strain; the tears lurk behind the laughter when the poet reveals his pain of spirit when under the savage strictures of a condemning Kirk and society. Sadly, one notes that the start of what Burns calls his dissipation is in reaction to the moral stance of his own father, whom he respected highly; the letter to John Moore paints the sad picture:

> In my seventeenth year, to give my manners a brush, I went to a country dancing-school. — My father had an unaccountable antipathy against these meetings; and my going was, what to this moment I repent, in opposition to his wishes. My father, as I said before, was subject to strong passions; from that instance of disobedience in me he took a sort of dislike to me, which I believe was one cause of the dissipation which marked my succeeding years. I say dissipation, comparatively with the strictness, and sobriety, and regularity of Presbyterian country life; for though the Will-o'-wisp meteors of thoughtless whim were almost the sole lights of my path, yet early ingrained piety and virtue kept me for several years afterwards within the line of innocence.

As with the poet's excessive drinking, one can perceive in Burns's sexual lapses the dichotomy between his ideals and his actual performance. Psychologically this is the same cyclic process of idealism, falling from the ideal to the real, then in reaction to the falling a regeneration of inspiration to express the dignity of ideal, independent existence.

It must be remembered that the Burns who faced the Kirk Session and who sat in the cutty stool was no unthinking brute but a sensitive poetic spirit ravaged by the degrading experience and almost maddened by it. There is tremendous courage in the Robert Burns who faced the Calvinistic censure of church and society at the very moment his heart was breaking. Consider in the light of these remarks the letter to John Arnot (April, 1786):

> How I bore this, can only be conceived. — All powers of recital labor far, far behind. — There is a pretty large portion of bedlam in the composition of a Poet at any time; but on this occasion I was nine parts & nine tenths, out of ten, stark staring mad. . . . My chained faculties broke loose; my maddening passions, roused to ten-fold fury, bore over their banks with impetuous, resistless force, carrying every check & principle before them — Counsel, was an unheeded call to the passing hurricane; Reason, a screaming elk in the vortex of Moskoestrom; & Religion, a feebly-struggling beaver down the roarings of Niagara. — I reprobated the first moment of my existence; execrated Adam's folly-infatuated wish for that goodly-looking, but poison-breathing, gift, which had ruined him, & undone me; & called on the womb of uncreated night to close over me & all my sorrows. . . . But this is not all. — Already the holy beagles, the houghmagandie pack, begin to snuff the scent, & I expect every moment to see them cast off, & hear them after me in full cry; but as I am an old fox, I shall give them dodging and doubling for it; & by and bye, I intend to earth among the mountains of Jamaica.

And telling John Moore of his friendship with Richard Brown, Burns reveals the total violation of his ideals in his begetting a bastard:

> He was the only man I ever saw who was a greater fool than myself, where woman was the presiding star; but he spoke of illicit love with the levity of a sailor, which hitherto I had regarded with horror. Here his friendship did me a mischief: and the consequence was, that soon after I resumed the plough, I wrote the *Poet's Welcome*.

Consonant with this serious side of the sexual question is Burns's attack on cynical seducers and sexual hypocrites. Alongside the over-painted sketch of the vile seducer in *The Cotter's Saturday Night* there is the sincere concluding stanza of *The Ruined Maid's Lament*:

> But deevil damn the lousy loun,
> Denies the bairn he got!
> Or lea's the merry a—e he lo'ed
> To wear a ragged coat!

The *Epistle to the Rev. John McMath*, addressed to a clergyman who preached against the Auld Light Calvinist doctrines, launches an attack on hypocrisy:

> God knows, I'm no the thing I shou'd be,
> Nor am I even the thing I cou'd be,
> But twenty times, I rather wou'd be
> An atheist clean,
> Than under gospel colors hid be
> Just for a screen.
>
> An honest man may like a glass,
> An honest man may like a lass,
> But mean revenge, an' malice fause
> He'll still disdain,
> An' then cry zeal for gospel laws,
> Like some we ken.
>
> They take religion in their mouth;
> They talk o' mercy, grace an' truth,
> For what? — to gie their malice skouth
> On some puir wight,
> An' hunt him down, o'er right an' ruth,
> To ruin streight.

And Burns's letter to Peter Hill (Ellisland, February 2nd, 1790) suggests a female revenge on 'those flinty-bosomed, puritannic Prosecutors of Female Frailty, & Persecutors of Female Charms' which comes straight out of *Lysistrata*.

As with Burns's treatment of the Devil and the drink, his dealing with the flesh is informed by the same essentially Scottish expression of universal attitudes. Burns as inspired poet has a wider range of physical and emotional experiences than the average man and indulges with a disconcerting, more than average zeal in the extremes of the range, but in the process he gives expression to a human failing which is ultimately less harshly to be judged than hypocrisy, lack of charity, greed, cruelty. How universal and yet how Scottish is Burns's summing up on the topic in his *Epistle to Captn. Willm. Logan at Park*:

> We've fauts an' failins, — granted clearly:
> We're frail, backsliding Mortals meerly:
> Eve's bonie Squad, Priests wyte them sheerly.
>   For our grand fa':
> But still — but still — I like them dearly;
>   God bless them a'!

Had he been asked to justify the discrepancy between his moral convictions and his worldly frailties, I am sure Burns would have given the same reply as the old Scottish minister chided by the Session for his drinking: 'Gentlemen, it's no the lamp ye follow, it's the licht.' This is exactly what the poet is told by his long-suffering Muse in the second Duan of *The Vision*:

> I saw thy pulse's maddening play,
> Wild-send thee Pleasure's devious way,
> Misled by Fancy's meteor-ray,
>   By passion driven;
> But yet the light that led astray,
>   Was light from Heaven.

10

Then wi' a rhyme or song he lash't 'em

We're a' dry wi' drinking o't,
We're a' dry wi' drinking o't:
The minister kisst the fidler's wife,
He could na preach for thinkin o't.

Aldous Huxley once said of Robert Burns, 'After Chaucer, Burns is the least pretentious and portentous; the most completely and harmoniously human of all English poets.' While Scots may not care for his attempt to claim their national poet for the opposition, Huxley is right to maintain that the universal appeal of Burns lies in the man's essential humanity. To be human is by very definition to be imperfect, and in this line of endeavour Burns has already been found quite expert. It follows, therefore, that Burns's attraction must lie in his giving to human imperfection an expression that is universal in its appeal, that (whatever its Scottish idiom) touches the heart of the common man everywhere. For me, Burns's humanity as enshrined in his poetry has two important sources, laughter and love — laughter, perhaps mortal man's best answer to the riddles of the universe, and love, certainly mortal man's only answer to the imperfection of this world and his only route to the perfection of eternity.

From quiet homes and first beginning,
Out to the undiscovered ends,
There's nothing worth the wear of winning,
But laughter and the love of friends.

Hilaire Belloc's *Dedicatory Ode* makes the same association of laughter and love, and finds in their combination the point of human existence. This is precisely why people without a sense of humour will never really understand the poetry of Burns, because in Burns the humourist and satirist is found much of the essential Robert Burns. In his poetry his laughter runs the entire gamut of humour, from the gentle laughter at human frailty in *Tam Glen* or *Duncan Gray* to the guffaws of *Sic a Wife as Willie's Wife*, to the drink and lust of *Tam o' Shanter* or *The Holy Fair*, to the satire of *Holy Willie's Prayer* and the *Address to the Unco Guid*. Yet this range in types is informed by one basic and underlying motif, gentle laughter at human weakness, gentle laughter born of the poet's ability always to see the humorous side, the human, forgiving side of every moral question. How gentle is the remonstrance to the girl who is unaware that a louse is crawling up the back of her proud, new bonnet, how gentle his excusing of the seduction in *The Jolly Beggars: A Cantata:*

> The Caird prevail'd — th' unblushing fair
> In his embraces sunk;
> Partly wi' Love o'ercome sae sair,
> An' partly she was drunk.

Without the laughter of love, how censorious and harsh would be a stern, Calvinistic judgment of the incident! For Burns and for the lover of Burns's poetry, laughter is essential to the appreciation of the nature of the human condition. As Frank Colby puts it (*Essays, I*), 'Men will confess to treason, murder, arson, false teeth, or a wig. How many of them will own up to a lack of humour?'

Initium sapientiae timor domini, students are reminded at Aberdeen University, 'The fear of the Lord is the beginning of wisdom.' The psalmist may very well be right, but the very next step towards wisdom is acquiring the ability to laugh first of all at oneself. This Burns does frequently and disarmingly, and nowhere better than in *The Vision*:

> All in this mottie, misty clime,
> I backward mus'd on wasted time,
> How I had spent my youthfu' prime,
>> An' done nae-thing,
> But stringing blethers up in rhyme
>> For fools to sing.
>
> Had I to guid advice but harket,
> I might, by this, hae led a market,
> Or strutted in a Bank and clarket
>> My Cash-Account;
> While here, half-mad, half-fed, half-sarket,
>> Is a' th' amount.

The poet, half-mad, half-fed, half-sarket, concludes logically that he must swear the obvious oath, 'That I, henceforth, would be *rhyme-*

proof Till my last breath,' but the door flies open and in the firelight
he sees his Muse Coila showing a little more leg than your average,
everyday Muse. The poet is instructed on how to be the Horace of
Nithsdale, but only after passing this vital test of self-assessment
through laughter:

> Down flow'd her robe, a tartan sheen,
> Till half a leg was scrimply seen;
> And such a leg! my bonie Jean
>   Could only peer it;
> Sae straught, sae taper, tight and clean,
>   Nane else came near it.

That the test is indeed vital is demonstrated by the former Archbishop
of Canterbury, Michael Ramsey. Delivering a series of eight public
addresses in the Sheldonian Theatre at Oxford in February, 1960, he
concluded the entire series with these words:

> If a man must be aware of himself it is a happy thing if he can
> *laugh at himself*, for that is a way of coming near to God.[37]

Once one has learned to laugh thus at oneself, and only then,
one is entitled to laugh at one's fellows. Burns can now proceed to
give the following picture of the ugly spouse of an unfortunate chap
in Dunscore, the nearest hamlet to Ellisland, in *Sic a Wife as Willie's
Wife*:

> She has an e'e, she has but ane,
>   Our cat has twa, the very colour;
> Five rusty teeth, forbye a stump,
>   A clapper-tongue wad deave a miller:
> A whiskin beard about her mou,
>   Her nose and chin they threaten ither;
> Sic a wife as Willie's wife,
>   I wad nae gie a button for her.

And Burns can now give the following picture of his famous antiquary
friend in his poem *On Captain Grose's Peregrinations Through Scotland:*

Hear, Land o' Cakes, and brither Scots,
Frae Maidenkirk to Johny Groats! —
If there's a hole in a' your coats,
        I rede you tent it:
A chiel's amang you, taking notes,
        An, faith, he'll prent it.

If in your bounds ye chance to light
Upon a fine, fat, fodgel wight,
O' stature short, but genius bright,
        That's he, mark weel —
And wow! he has an unco slight
        O' cauk and keel.

By some auld, houlet-haunted biggin,
Or kirk deserted by its riggin,
It's ten to ane ye'll find him snug in
        Some eldritch part,
Wi' deils, they say, Lord safe's! colleaguin
        At some black art.

Very popular in Burns's century were the telling rejoinder and admiration for those quick enough of wit to practice such verbal riposte, most people finding adequate rejoinder coming to the tongue about ten minutes too late to be effective. Instead of the usual examples from the acid tongue of Dr. Johnson, here is the record of a brief encounter won by John Wilkes (1727-97):

THE EARL OF SANDWICH: 'Egad, sir, I do not know whether
        you will die on the gallows or of
        the pox.
JOHN WILKES: 'That will depend, my Lord, on whether I
        embrace your principles or your mistress.'

Such verbal fencing had been dear to the Scottish heart for centuries, of course, an early instance being offered in the ninth century when Joannes Scotus Erigena dined not wisely but too well across the table from Charles the Bald of France:

KING CHARLES: *Quid distat inter Scotum et sottum?* 'What
        is the difference between a Scot and a sot?'
JOHN THE SCOT: *Mensa tantum,* 'Just a table's width.'

And one comes right up to date with the conversation between an old Scottish farmer and the English tourist whose car has just squashed the farmer's rooster:

ENGLISH TOURIST: 'I say, old chap, I'm frightfully sorry, but I seem to have run over your rooster. I'd like to replace him.'
SCOTTISH FARMER: 'Suit yersel — the hens is roun' the back.'

Burns, of course, was adept at poking fun of this variety. One day in Carlisle, he allowed his horse, Jenny Geddes, to wander into a field belonging to the town, and the mayor had the animal placed in custody. When informed of the name of the beast's owner, the mayor ordered its release with words which prompted a notable reply from the poet:

MAYOR OF CARLISLE: 'Let him have it, by all means, or the circumstances will be heard of for ages to come.'
ROBERT BURNS: 'Was e'er puir poet sae befitted?
The maister drunk, — the horse committed:
Puir harmless beast! tak' thee nae care,
Thou'lt be a horse when he's nae mair!'

In similar vein is his *Epitaph on a Wag in Mauchline*:

Lament 'im Mauchline husbands a',
    He aften did assist ye;
For had ye staid whole weeks awa'
    Your wives they ne'er had miss'd ye.

Ye Mauchline bairns as on ye pass,
    To school in bands thegither,
O tread ye lightly on his grass,
    Perhaps he was your father.

In *Last May a Braw Wooer*, a blonde beauty is annoyed when her lover takes up with her raven-haired cousin temporarily and then wishes to return to his earlier amour. Here follows the girl's account of the swain's proposal and her riposte:

> But owre my left shouther I gae him a blink,
>   Least neebors might say I was saucy:
> My wooer he caper'd as he'd been in drink,
>   And vow'd I was his dear lassie, dear lassie,
>   And vow'd I was his dear lassie.
>
> I spier'd for my cousin fu' couthy and sweet,
>   Gin she had recover'd her hearin,
> And how her new shoon fit her auld shachl't feet;
>   But, heavens! how he fell a swearin, a swearin,
>   But, heavens! how he fell a swearin!

For the creative artist, critics and reviewers are fair targets for barbed shafts, and Burns finds it difficult to refrain from counterblast in his extempore lines on returning a newspaper containing criticisms of his works *To Captain Riddel, of Glenriddel*:

> Your News and Review, Sir, I've read through and
>   through, Sir,
>   With little admiring or blaming:
> The Papers are barren of home-news or foreign,
>   No murders or rapes worth the naming.
>
> Our friends the Reviewers, those Chippers and
>   Hewers,
>   Are judges of Mortar and Stone, Sir;
> But of meet, or unmeet, in a Fabrick complete,
>   I'll boldly pronounce they are none, Sir.

Burns would no doubt have sympathised with the composer who addressed himself thus to one of his tormentors:

> Dear sir: I am seated in the smallest room of my home. Your review is before me. Shortly it will be behind me. Very truly yours . . .[38]

Burns offers the following picture of the poet writing under the reviewers' whips in his *Third Epistle to Robert Graham, Esq., of Fintry*:

> Vampyre booksellers drain him to the heart,
> And scorpion Critics cureless venom dart.

Critics — appalled, I venture on the name,
Those cut-throat bandits in the paths of fame:
Bloody dissectors, worse than ten Monroes;
He hacks to teach, they mangle to expose.

His heart by causeless wanton malice wrung,
By blockheads' daring into madness stung;
His well-won bays, than life itself more dear,
By miscreants torn, who ne'er one sprig must wear:
Foiled, bleeding, tortured, in the unequal strife,
The hapless Poet flounders on thro' life;
Till fled each hope that once his bosom fired,
And fled each Muse that glorious once inspired,
Low-sunk in squalid, unprotected age,
Dead, even resentment, for his injured page,
He heeds or feels no more the ruthless Critic's rage!

In the hands of the true artist, laughter does more than entertain, for it has a strong moral force behind it. When I maintain that
the tone appropriate for the Immortal Memory is in part humorous,
I do so not only because in Burns's humour one finds the essence of
Scottish humour and thereby asserts one's Scottishness annually to
the world but also because in Burns's humour one finds his serious
moral statements. When to laughter is added irony, one gets that
highly moral force, satire; when to laughter is added irony and love,
one gets satire of the best kind, satire laced with humour and informed
by a sense of balance that will never become lost.

Satire by its very nature implies an ideal society (or at least a
human society ordered along right and moral lines) while poking fun
at man's actual society which falls so far short of the desired norm.
By making people laugh at what is undesirable the satirist hopes to
move them to emend their behaviour along the lines he implies. Sati-
rists fail when they lose their sense of balance, that is, when they
become too angry or bitter to be funny any longer — witness *Gulliver's Travels*, especially the last voyage of Gulliver, that to the land of
the Houyhnhnms. Burns's sense of humour does not fail him, and this
is why in the satires is encountered a poet who has strong feelings of
right and wrong and of love for his fellow man but who never loses his
sense of balance because of his ability always to see the humorous
side and the human, forgiving side of every moral question. Satire is
that most moral of poetic forms intended not to hurt as sarcasm can

but to emend behaviour through laughter. Examples include *The Holy Fair, Holy Willie's Prayer, To A Louse* and *The Twa Dogs*:

> By this, the sun was out o' sight,
> An' darker gloamin brought the night:
> The bum-clock humm'd wi' lazy drone,
> The kye stood rowtan i' the loan;
> When up they gat, an' shook their lugs,
> Rejoic'd they were na men but dogs;
> An' each took aff his several way,
> Resolv'd to meet some ither day.

One can sense that if in certain moods Burns would agree with Byron in *Don Juan* that 'Man, being reasonable, must get drunk,' he would not agree that dissipation can be separated from its reckoning, as Byron suggests:

> Let us have wine and women, mirth and laughter,
> Sermons and soda-water the day after.

With Burns, the sin and its correction coincide. Even in a poem of pure humour such as *Tam o' Shanter*, the ideal lurks clearly behind the real. When in the opening scene in the pub the reader is told that the reaming swats 'drank divinely', he is put on his guard for a contrast between the values of the public house and the values of the church, a contrast immediately implied in the description of the relationship between Tam and his friend Johnny:

> And at his elbow, Souter Johnny,
> His ancient, trusty, drouthy crony;
> Tam lo'ed him like a vera brither;
> They had been fou for weeks thegither.

The last line quoted underlines the spurious nature of the brotherly love of Tam and Johnny, a love born in the alcoholic environment of the pub in place of true brotherly love founded on Christian moral bases. Of a similarly false, though temporarily beguiling, nature are the barmaid's warmth, the landlord's laugh and Tam's feeling glorious, 'O'er a' the ills o' life victorious!' The voice of offended true morality interrupts the poem in the ecclesiastical tones of the church literally to pour cold water on the spurious warmth of the bar environment:

> But pleasures are like poppies spread,
> You seize the flower, its bloom is shed;
> Or like the snow falls in the river,
> A moment white — then melts for ever;
> Or like the borealis race,
> That flit ere you can point their place;
> Or like the rainbow's lovely form
> Evanishing amid the storm.

The contrast between the ale-house values and those of true morality informs such a poem as *The Holy Fair*. Like Macbeth on the blasted heath meeting the three Norns, the poet on the moors of Galston (the parish next to that of Mauchline) encounters three hags named Fun, Superstition and Hypocrisy who are on their way to a holy fair at Mauchline. The poet joins in the revels of the supposedly serious, spiritual occasion of a type common in Scotland a couple of centuries ago; a fair is to be held out of doors between the pub and the church so that ministers and elders from several parishes may preach in the open air to their assembled congregations. The flocks have their own, less spiritually elevated motives in attending the holy fair, as Burns makes clear:

> Here, stands a shed to find the show'rs,
>   An' screen our countra Gentry;
> There, Racer-Jess, an' twathree whores,
>   Are blinkan at the entry:
> Here sits a raw o' tittlan jads,
>   Wi' heaving breasts an' bare neck,
> An' there, a batch o' Wabster lads,
>   Blackguarding frae Kilmarnock,
>   For fun this day.

The various ministers present the less immediately attractive wares the church has on offer. Moodie of Riccarton preaches damnation in terms that would frighten even the Devil himself:

> Should Hornie, as in ancient days,
>   'Mang sons o' God present him,
> The vera sight o' Moodie's face,
>   To 's ain het hame had sent him
>   Wi' fright that day.

Moodie's act proves too hard for the moderate Smith of Galston to follow, with his moderate views and English style, and the crowd deserts to the pub:

> Smith opens out his cauld harangues,
>   On practice and on morals;
> An' aff the godly pour in thrangs,
>   To gie the jars an' barrels
>   A lift that day.

Peebles of Newton-upon-Ayr and Wee Miller (later of Kilmaurs) present their gloomy views on life and religion, but it takes Black Russell of the chapel of ease, Kilmarnock, to rouse the revellers with strong whiffs of brimstone in a stentorian voice bellowing into the utmost recesses of the pub. 'But now the Lord's ain trumpet touts,' says Burns, altering Isaiah to permit the paronomasia of 'touts' and thereby contrast the sound of the trump with the clink of the glasses. Black Russell holds his congregation over the very brink of Hell itself in an attempt to awaken the flock to true values as he sees them:

> A vast, unbottom'd, boundless Pit,
>   Fill'd fou o' lowan brunstane,
> Whase raging flame, an' scorching heat,
>   Wad melt the hardest whunstane!
> The half-asleep start up wi' fear,
>   An' think they hear it roaran,
> When presently it does appear,
>   'Twas but some neebor snoran
>   Asleep that day.

The congregation are asleep because of excesses of drink and pleasure rather than because of excesses of true religion and true morality. Yet the irony is subtler than this, for true religion and true morality are also asleep themselves, and do not waken because of the roaring of Black Russell and his compeers; true values are not to be found in stern and ostentatious Calvinism in Mauchline kirkyard any more than they are to be found in Poosie Nansie's ale-house. At the end of the poem, a humanity unconverted and unrepentant departs to indulge in the many weaknesses to which flesh is heir, for such is the mortal condition of which the poet in his humour and love is gently tolerant:

> How monie hearts this day converts,
>   O' Sinners and o' Lasses!
> Their hearts o' stane, gin night are gane
>   As saft as only flesh is.
> There's some are fou o' love divine;
>   There's some are fou o' brandy;
> An' monie jobs that day begin,
>   May end in Houghmagandie
>   Some ither day.

The Holy Fair earned the poet the censure of the church he
satirised, needless to say, and he did nothing to redeem himself in
ecclesiastical eyes in his *Journal of a Tour in the Highlands:*

> What a poor, pimping business is a Presbyterean place of worship,
> dirty, narrow and squalid, stuck in a corner of old Popish grandeur
> such as Linlithgow and much more Melrose! ceremony and show,
> if judiciously thrown in, absolutely necessary for the bulk of man-
> kind; both in religious & civil matters.

The genesis of Burns's attack on the church in *Holy Willie's
Prayer* and *Epitaph on Holy Willie* was the onslaught on the poet's
friend Gavin Hamilton by William Fisher, a Mauchline farmer and
church elder, because Hamilton had paid a beggar to work in his
garden on a Sunday. Burns savages the hypocritical Willie in defence
of his patron in *Holy Willie's Prayer*, continuing the same train of
thought in the *Epitaph* written after the real Willie was found dead,
drunken in a ditch. In *Holy Willie's Prayer*, of course, Willie is used
to represent the values of Auld Licht Calvinism, and the poem's attack
is not restricted to the individual, as is made clear by the opening
stanza's smug account of predestination:

> O Thou that in the heavens does dwell!
> Wha, as it pleases best thysel,
> Sends ane to heaven and ten to hell,
>   A' for thy glory!
> And no for ony gude or ill
>   They've done before thee.

Willie is overheard in prayer as in a dramatic interior mono-
logue he lays bare his petty soul. His pettiness and hypocrisy arise
from the values of Calvinism as he understand it, a Calvinism that

casts God in its own image through the doctrine of predestination. Such a doctrine is satisfying to those who can convince themselves that they are of the elect and can therefore do no wrong, and such a doctrine gives rise very easily to hypocrisy as the self-righteous, self-styled elect pat themselves on the back:

> Yet I am here, a chosen sample,
> To shew thy grace is great and ample:
> I'm here, a pillar o' thy temple
>   Strong as a rock,
> A guide, a ruler and example
>   To a' thy flock.

As one of the chosen in God's chosen race, Willie in his role of elder reprimands those who drink and swear and sing and dance, yet himself commits the act of fornication, in Calvinist eyes the surest way to eternal damnation. The hypocrite proudly confesses his sins:

> But yet — O Lord — confess I must —
> At times I'm fash'd wi' fleshly lust;
> And sometimes too, in wardly trust
>   Vile Self gets in;
> But thou remembers we are dust,
>   Defil'd wi' sin.

I am sure God values the reminder from his very far from contrite elder as much as he did overhearing the Calvinist preacher who began his sermon with the words, 'The Lord has said — and *rightly* said — . . .'

Willie now attempts to bargain with the Deity for forgiveness on his own, debased, petty terms:

> O Lord — yestreen — thou kens — wi' Meg —
> Thy pardon I sincerely beg!
> O may't ne'er be a living plague,
>   To my dishonor!
> And I'll ne'er lift a lawless leg
>   Again upon her.

The hypocrite now seeks to get a special rate from God for buying absolution for fornication in bulk:

Holy Willie's Grave, Mauchline

> Besides, I farther maun avow,
> Wi' Lizie's lass, three times — I trow — —
> But Lord, that Friday I was fou
>   When I cam near her;
> Or else, thou kens, thy servant true
>   Wad never steer her.

'Fornication? But that was in another country, and besides, the wench is dead.' This is the protest of the villain Barabas in *The Jew of Malta*, not the contrite confession and prayer for repentance of an elder of the church. Willie pays no compliment to his lady-love when he protests that he did his stuff only on a Friday night when he was drunken, and only half a compliment to his God when he implies that he did his stuff three times, once for each member of the Trinity. Willie smugly concludes that his taste for fornication is a thorn in his side placed there by God as a reminder lest Willie be too proud of his election.

Convinced that he can have the best of both worlds, fornication and forgiveness, Willie pettily turns to curse his enemies, particularly those who like Gavin Hamilton lead the populace in laughter, the one torment a hypocrite cannot abide. Hamilton's garden, whose care started the two men on their collision course, must be marked out for a special cursing like the ungodly cursed by Jehovah in Deuteronomy 28.15-19:

> Lord mind Gaun Hamilton's deserts!
> He drinks, and swears, and plays at cartes,
> Yet has sae mony taking arts
> > Wi' Great and Sma',
> Frae God's ain priest the people's hearts
> > He steals awa.
>
> And when we chasten'd him therefore,
> Thou kens how he bred sic a splore,
> And set the warld in a roar
> > O' laughin at us:
> Curse thou his basket and his store,
> > Kail and potatoes.

After closing maledictions on all his foes, Willie returns to his basic supposition that he is on earth 'for gifts and grace' and concludes complacently on the same impertinent note on which he began:

> But Lord, remember me and mine
> Wi' mercies temporal and divine!
> That I for grace and gear may shine,
> > Excell'd by nane!
> And a' the glory shall be thine!
> > Amen! Amen!

Willie's prayer is thus an awful parody of the prayers in the Presbyterian order of service: prayer of approach to God; prayer of adoration, confession, assurance of pardon; ascription of praise; prayer of thanksgiving, intercession, petition; benediction and Amen. There is nothing left for the critic to say, for Willie himself has stripped his petty soul bare before his audience. There is just one way to deal with such complacent people as Willie or the cruel rich people of *The Twa Dogs* and that is to satirize them as Burns does, through satire to imply the essential dignity of the poor and to show concern for the down-trodden of the world.

Similar poise is shown in *The Twa Dogs*, in which there is a dialogue between a rich dog and a poor one. Burns shows his real concern for the down-trodden of this world and his anger at the effects of the division of society upon the individual by maintaining the humorous guise absolutely. How the poet's spirit must have writhed to watch his father's treatment at the hands of the cruel factor, as described in the letter to Moore:

> My father's generous master died; the farm proved a ruinous bargain; and, to clench the misfortune, we fell into the hands of a factor, who sat for the picture I have drawn of one in my *Tale of Twa Dogs*. . . . A novel-writer might perhaps have viewed these scenes with some satisfaction; but so did not I; my indignation yet boils at the recollection of the scoundrel factor's insolent threatening letters, which used to set us all in tears.

But these feelings are sublimated through satire into the speech of the dog Caesar:

> I've notic'd, on our Laird's court-day,
> An' mony a time my heart's been wae,
> Poor tenant-bodies, scant o' cash,
> How they maun thole a factor's snash;
> He'll stamp an' threaten, curse an' swear,
> He'll apprehend them, poind their gear,
> While they maun stand, wi' aspect humble,
> An' hear it a', an' fear an' tremble!
>
> I see how folk live that hae riches,
> But surely poor-folk maun be wretches!

And Luath replies with dignity:

> They're no sae wretched 's ane wad think;
> Tho' constantly on poortith's brink,
> The're sae accustom'd wi' the sight,
> The view o't gies them little fright.

If men were talking, this would break the heart, but Burns is careful to maintain the balance through laughter, to remind one that these are dogs talking:

> When up they gat, an' shook their lugs,
> Rejoic'd they were na men but dogs. . .

And now the ultimate point of laughter in Burns's scheme of things is clear. Laughter is the great leveller which merges social ranks, which cuts away all hypocrisy and studied pomp, which deflates the bubble pride, which makes love warm, which makes adversity tolerable, which wards off the slings and arrows of outrageous fortune, and which wipes away the tear whose sorrow would else break the heart. It is therefore without surprise that one finds Burns forgiving and understanding even the unco guid in his *Address to the Unco Guid, or the Rigidly Righteous*:

> Then gently scan your brother Man,
> Still gentler sister Woman;
> Tho' they may gang a kennin wrang,
> To step aside is human:
> One point must still be greatly dark,
> The moving Why they do it;
> And just as lamely can ye mark,
> How far perhaps they rue it.

> Who made the heart, 'tis He alone
> Decidedly can try us,
> He knows each chord its various tone,
> Each spring its various bias:
> Then at the balance let's be mute,
> We never can adjust it;
> What's done we partly may compute,
> But know not what's resisted.

To describe Robert Burns as the poet of laughter is thus to find in him his greatest strength, to pay him the supreme compliment, and to pin-point part of the source of his universal appeal.

11
But ay a heart aboon them a'

If Heaven a draught of heavenly pleasure spare,
One cordial in this melancholy Vale,
'Tis when a youthful, loving, modest Pair,
In other's arms, breathe out the tender tale,
Beneath the milk-white thorn that scents the ev'ning gale.

Detail from Burns Statue, Ayr

Burns expounds his approach to the composition of his songs in two letters to Thomson (September, 1793):

> You know that my pretensions to musical taste are merely a few of nature's instincts, untaught and untutored by art. For this reason, many musical compositions . . . affect my simple lug no otherwise than merely as melodious din. On the other hand, by way of amends, I am delighted with many little melodies, which

133

the learned musician despises as silly and insipid . . . until I am complete master of a tune, in my own singing, (such as it is) I can never compose for it. My way is: I consider the poetic sentiment correspondent to my idea of the musical expression; then choose my theme; begin one stanza; when that is composed, which is generally the most difficult part of the business, I walk out, sit down now and then, look out for objects in nature around me that are in unison and harmony with the cogitations of my fancy, and workings of my bosom; humming every now and then the air, with the verses I have framed. When I feel my Muse beginning to jade, I retire to the solitary fireside of my study, and there commit my effusions to paper.

The poet of the laughter of love takes a rightful place in the first rank of love poets, earning that place on the basis of the virtually universal acclaim accorded such songs as *Auld Lang Syne, Ye Banks and Braes o' Bonie Doon, Ca' The Yowes, Ae Fond Kiss, Bonie Wee Thing, Afton Water, O My Luve's Like a Red, Red Rose, Green Grow the Rashes O* and *The Lea-Rig*. Without a McKellar present to sing these songs, any discussion in cold print of the songs without their accompanying music must of necessity constitute an inadequate artificiality; yet no consideration of Robert Burns can be complete without attention being paid to the songs, for in this sphere he excels.

For Robert Burns, 'song' and 'love' were so closely related as to be to all intents and purposes synonyms. The close association of these terms is no accident in his account in the letter to John Moore of the genesis of his first love song in 1773, when the poet 'first committed the sin of Ryme' (Mauchline, August 2nd, 1787):

Among her other love-inspiring qualities, she sung sweetly; and it was her favourite reel, to which I attempted giving an embodied vehicle in rhyme . . . Thus with me began love and poetry.

The song of which Burns talks here is 'Handsome Nell':

A gaudy dress and gentle air
    May slightly touch the heart,
But it's innocence and modesty
    That polishes the dart.

'Tis this in Nelly pleases me,
    'Tis this enchants my soul;
For absolutely in my breast
    She reigns without controul.

Writing in his *Commonplace Book* in August, 1783, Burns talks of the same song in the same clear terms:

> There is certainly some connection between Love, and Music & Poetry . . . For my own part I never had the least thought or inclination of turning Poet till I got once heartily in Love, and then Rhyme & Song were, in a manner, the spontaneous language of my heart.

The spontaneous overflow of the powerful emotion of love bore fruit in the songs in the Kilmarnock and Edinburgh Editions, in *The Jolly Beggars: A Cantata* and *The Merry Muses of Caledonia*, and in the collections compiled in collaboration with James Johnson and George Thomson. To Johnson's *The Scots Musical Museum* Burns contributed about sixty songs of his own, and Thomson's *A Select Collection of Original Scottish Airs* contains a hundred of Burns's original songs. Burns made more reputation than hard cash from his work of collection and composition, as he records in his letter to Thomson (Dumfries, September 16, 1792):

> As to any remuneration, you may think my songs either above or below price; for they shall absolutely be the one or the other. In the honest enthusiasm with which I embark in your undertaking, to talk of money, wages, fee, hire, &c. would be downright *prostitution of soul*! A proof of each of the Songs that I compose or amend, I shall receive as a favour.

Nevertheless, Burns could have used more than the few complimentary copies and £10 which he received from Thomson.

The key to the song collections is Burns's remark above, 'Songs that I compose or amend', for he not only wrote songs of his own for the collections but in a vast labour of love gathered from all possible sources ancient Scottish lyrics and tunes which he 'amended' wherever necessary. The attitude is made clear in the preface to the second volume of *The Scots Musical Museum*:

> . . . the Collection is meant to be solely the music of our own Country — The Songs contained in this Volume, both music and poetry, are all of them the work of Scotsmen — Wherever the old words could be recovered, they have been preferred; both as generally suiting better the genius of the tunes, and to preserve the productions of those earlier Sons of the Scottish Muses, some of whose names deserved a better fate than has befallen them — 'Buried 'midst the wreck of things which were.'

Scrupulous though Burns may have been in his attempts to give credit to others whenever it was due, there is no doubt that his editing and rewriting, his adaptation and reforging of older material have put the imprint of his genius on all the songs, making them indubitably his own. Nevertheless, one ought to bear in mind that not all the words of all the songs are *originally* by Burns while at the same time giving him the major credit he deserves. A case in point is that most Burnsian of all Burns songs, *Auld Lang Syne*, of which stanzas two and three are by Burns and the others are from an 'old song of the olden times, and which has never been in print, nor even in manuscript, until I took it down from an old man's singing — Light be the turf on the breast of the Heaven-inspired poet who composed this glorious fragment!'[39]

Another instance is *Ca' The Yowes*, which Burns sent to Thomson with the following note (September, 1794):

> I am flattered at your adopting, *Ca' the yowes to the knowes*, as it was owing to me that ever it saw the light. About seven years ago I was well acquainted with a worthy little fellow of a clergyman, a Mr. Clunie, who sung it charmingly; and, at my request, Mr. Clarke took it down from his singing. When I gave it to Johnson, I added some stanzas to the song, and mended others, but still it will not do for you. In a solitary stroll which I took to-day, I tried my hand on a few pastoral lines, following up the idea of the chorus, which I would preserve. Here it is, with all its crudities and imperfections on its head.

> Ca' the yowes to the knowes,
> Ca' them whare the heather grows,
> Ca' them whare the burnie rowes,
>   My bonie Dearie.

> Hark, the mavis' evening sang
> Sounding Clouden's woods amang;
> Then a faulding let us gang,
>   My bonie Dearie.

> We'll gae down by Clouden side,
> Through the hazels spreading wide
> O'er the waves, that sweetly glide
>   To the moon sae clearly.

> Yonder Clouden's silent towers,
> Where at moonshine midnight hours
> O'er the dewy bending flowers
> Fairies dance sae cheary.
>
> Ghaist nor bogle shalt thou fear;
> Thou'rt to Love and Heaven sae dear,
> Nocht of Ill may come thee near,
> My bonie Dearie.
>
> Fair and lovely as thou art,
> Thou hast stown my very heart;
> I can die — but canna part,
> My bonie Dearie.

Bearing in mind, then, that not every word of every song is by Burns, and conceding that to discuss the lyrics in isolation and divorced from their music is to consider only part of the total artistic effect of a given song, I think one may, nevertheless, justifiably take the lyrics of Burns's love-songs along with his love poems in an attempt to trace the second element of the 'laughter of love' formula for the poet's universal appeal. The artistic purpose is identical, the unchanged subject remains the pleasure and pain of human life and love, and the value of the laughter persists in its proximity to tears. Burns notes in his *Commonplace Book* in September, 1785:

> . . . as I hope my poor, country Muse, who, all rustic, akward, and unpolished as she is, has more charms for me than any other of the pleasures of life beside — as I hope she will not then desert me, I may . . . learn to be, if not happy, at least easy, and south a sang to sooth my misery.

In Burns's love poetry, the laughter is complemented by lyricism, the quality which gently extracts from the things of everyday that which is eternal in all its poignancy. Consider, for instance, the touching simplicity and pathos of the sad girl's farewell to her Jacobite lover who must leave for permanent exile across the sea:

> The sodger frae the wars returns,
> The sailor frae the main;
> But I hae parted frae my Love,
> Never to meet again, my dear,
> Never to meet again.

> When day is gane, and night is come,
> And a' folk bound to sleep;
> I think on him that's far awa,
> The lee-lang night and weep, my dear,
> The lee-lang night and weep.

The poignancy produced by the poet's unerring poise and simplicity of lyrical utterance brings the tear to the eye. The breaking heart is full of feeling.

The laughter is still present in the love poetry, as can be seen in the poetic expression Burns gives to his relationship with his wife, Bonnie Jean, Jean Armour. In his letters, Burns speaks of marriage as follows (to Gavin Hamilton? Dumfries, July 16th, 1793):

> Oh, there is nothing like matrimony for setting a man's face Zion-ward; whether it be that it sublimates a man above the visible diurnal sphere, or whether it tires him of this sublunary state, or whether the delicious morsel of happiness which he enjoys in the conjugal yoke gives him a longing for the feasts above, or whether a poor husband thinks he has every chance in his favor, as, should he go to hell, he can be no worse — I shall leave to a weel-waled Presbytery of orthodox Ayrshire priests to determine.

O That I had Ne'er Been Married is a song whose joking tone matches that of *I Hae A Wife o' My Ain*:

> I hae a wife o' my ain,
> I'll partake wi' naebody;
> I'll tak Cuckold frae nane,
> I'll gie Cuckold to naebody.

One need read no further to know that the tongue is in the cheek! In similar appraisal of wedlock, Burns writes to Alexander Cunningham (Dumfries, September 10th, 1792):

> Apropos! How do you like, I mean *really* like, the married life? Ah, my friend! matrimony is quite a different thing from what your love-sick youths and sighing girls take it to be! But marriage, we are told, is appointed by God, and I shall never quarrel with any of his institutions.

Yet Burns addressed some of his tenderest poems to Jean, whom he truly loved and with whom he had a large family, four boys and a girl; a fifth boy was born a few days after the poet's death. It was to his Bonnie Jean that the poet wrote the exquisite honeymoon poem *Of A' The Airts The Wind Can Blaw* with its touching opening stanza:

Of a' the airts the wind can blaw,
I dearly like the West;
For there the bony Lassie lives,
The Lassie I lo'e best:
Theres wild-woods grow, and rivers row,
And mony a hill between;
But day and night my fancy's flight
Is ever wi' my Jean.

When Jean finally came to the poet's house as his wife, it was to be welcomed with the following charming lyric:

O were I on Parnassus hill;
Or had o' Helicon my fill;
That I might catch poetic skill,
To sing how dear I love thee.
But Nith maun be my Muses well,
My Muse maun be thy bonie sel;
On Corsincon I'll glowr and spell,
And write how dear I love thee.

Then come, sweet Muse, inspire my lay!
For a' the lee-lang simmer's day,
I couldna sing, I couldna say,
How much, how dear, I love thee.
I see thee dancing o'er the green,
Thy waist sae jimp, thy limbs sae clean,
Thy tempting lips, thy roguish een —
By Heaven and Earth I love thee.

By night, by day, a-field, at hame,
The thoughts o' thee my breast inflame;
And ay I muse and sing thy name,
I only live to love thee.
Tho' I were doomed to wander on,
Beyond the sea, beyond the sun,
Till my last, weary sand was run;
Till then — and then I love thee.

So perfect is the poise, so great the control of simplicity, that one has no trouble in accepting the closing hyperboles about the infinities of time and distance throughout which his true love will endure.

In the eyes of many, Burns's supreme achievement consists in the hauntingly beautiful and tender love-poems such as *The Farewell, O Wert Thou in the Cauld Blast, Canst Thou Leave Me Thus, My Katy?* and *The Bonie Wee Thing*:

> Bonie wee thing, canie wee thing,
>   Lovely wee thing, wert thou mine,
> I wad wear thee in my bosom,
>   Lest my Jewel I should tine.

No-one of any sentiment can listen dry of eye to Sylvander's parting from Clarinda in *Ae Fond Kiss*:

> Had we never lov'd sae kindly,
> Had we never lov'd sae blindly!
> Never met — or never parted,
> We had ne'er been broken-hearted.
>
> Fare-thee-weel, thou first and fairest!
> Fare-thee-weel, thou best and dearest!
> Thine be ilka joy and treasure,
> Peace, Enjoyment, Love, and Pleasure!
>
> Ae fond kiss, and then we sever!
> Ae fareweel, Alas, for ever!
> Deep in heart-wrung tears I'll pledge thee,
> Warring sighs and groans I'll wage thee.

Burns the poet of nature finds all her forces gathered in his support when he talks of his love. In *Bonie Bell*, the Spring, the waters, the sunny skies, morning and evening, all creatures, all flowers, all seasons rejoice with the poet in his love for his Bonie Bell, and in *Afton Water* a similarly anthropomorphic view of nature is taken when the poet conspires with the gently-flowing river, the sweet-singing birds, the neighbouring hills, mild evening and the sweet-scented flowers not to disturb his Mary:

> Flow gently, sweet Afton, among thy green braes,
> Flow gently, sweet River, the theme of my lays;
> My Mary's asleep by thy murmuring stream,
> Flow gently, sweet Afton, disturb not her dream.

All nature again can be sensed approving in the background when in the gloaming the poet sets out to meet his ain kind dearie on *The Lea-Rig*:

> When o-er the hill the eastern star
>   Tells bughtin-time is near, my jo,
> And owsen frae the furrowed field
>   Return sae dowf and weary O:
> Down by the burn where scented birks
>   Wi' dew are hanging clear, my jo,
> I'll meet thee on the lea-rig,
>   My ain kind Dearie O.

Note here the precision of the writing; any who think poetry vague and artificial lose in argument with those who cite Burns as an example of artistic control. Here, without learned quotations from the Classics, arcane rhyming schemes, sesquipedalian rhetoric, Burns paints a nature picture of the sublimest simplicity. The star, the oxen, the dew tell the poet that the time for his rendezvous is at hand. One sees the star peeping over the hill, one sees the furrows of the field lit by the deep-shadowing light of the setting sun. One hears the sheep bleating, the oxen lowing, the burn murmuring, the birches rustling in the breeze. One smells the birches' heady scent, intensified by the dew. All the natural senses are precisely stirred, in the sights, the smells, the acoustics of evening in the countryside, and the natural world and the poet are ready for the tender warmth of love. Such poise is exquisite.

Burns's lyrical gift gives him the necessary poise to welcome his illegitimate daughter into the world in 1784 in the poem *A Poet's Welcome to his Love-Begotten Daughter*. His defiance of the Kirk Session and his disregard of the gossips go hand in hand with a moving confession and a warm welcome into a troublous world:

> Lord grant that thou may ay inherit
> Thy Mither's looks an' gracefu' merit;
> An' thy poor, worthless Daddie's spirit,
>   Without his failins!
> 'Twad please me mair to see thee heir it
>   Than stocked mailins!

> For if thou be, what I wad hae thee,
> And tak the counsel I shall gie thee,
> I'll never rue my trouble wi' thee,
> The cost nor shame o't,
> But be a loving Father to thee,
> And brag the name o't.

More touching yet are the sad little poems on the deaths of some of his children, poems in which the tears are kept below the surface by sheer poetic strength. Consider first *On the Death of a Favourite Child*, a poem written about the death of a little daughter when the poet was away from home. The closing stanzas run thus:

> My child, thou are gone to the home of thy rest,
> Where suffering no longer can harm thee:
> Where the songs of the Good, where the hymns of
> the Blest
> Through an endless existence shall charm thee!
>
> While he, thy fond parent, must sighing sojourn
> Through the dire desert regions of sorrow,
> O'er the hope and misfortune of being to mourn,
> And sigh for his life's latest morrow.[40]

On the Poet's Daughter, Who Died 1795 uses the image for the child of a rose yet in the bud, a rose which in this case will never come to the full and joyous bloom of summer but must remain for ever a promise never to be realised — in this world, that is:

> Here lies a rose, a budding rose,
> Blasted before its bloom;
> Whose innocence did sweets disclose
> Beyond that flower's perfume.
>
> To those who for her loss are grieved,
> This consolation's given —
> She's from a world of woe relieved,
> And blooms, a rose, in Heaven.[41]

The image of the rose, in happier application, begins one of the most beautiful love songs ever written, *O My Luve's Like a Red, Red Rose*. The poem is not too copious to quote in full, and it were sacrilegious to abbreviate it:

> O my Luve's like a red, red rose,
> That's newly sprung in June;
> O my Luve's like the melodie
> That's sweetly play'd in tune.
>
> As fair art thou, my bonie lass,
> So deep in love am I;
> And I will love thee still, my Dear,
> Till a' the seas gang dry.
>
> Till a' the seas gang dry, my Dear,
> And the rocks melt wi' the sun:
> I will love thee still, my Dear,
> While the sands o' life shall run.
>
> And fare thee weel, my only Luve!
> And fare thee weel, a while!
> And I will come again, my Luve,
> Tho' it were ten thousand mile!

This exquisite lyric one must not let the critics destroy with tedious analysis or belie with false compare. There is no need to *analyse* the poet's simplicity by pointing out that of 109 words, only 7 are not monosyllables, nor is there need to compare the poem to Catullus' *Vivamus, mea Lesbia, atque Amemus*, for the suave complexity of the Roman poet's love lyric operates on quite a different plane from Burns's song. Suffice it to note the simple but beautiful imagery which leads from a single, fragile flower to the infinite time and infinite distances of the second part of the poem. Burns's symbol of love is the gentle rose, the sweet spring promise of summer glory to come, and the singer's love grows and blossoms as the rose until it can be compared to nothing less than infinity. Here is the ploughman-poet come into his own, rising in spirit above the barren soil of Mossgiel to pluck a precious bloom from the very fields of Elysium.

Most touching of all, perhaps, are Burns's poems to his Highland Mary, Mary Campbell. Such poems as *To Mary* or *The Highland Lassie* show the depth of feeling with which Burns contemplated his imminent departure for the West Indies in 1786 and his parting for ever from his Highland Mary:

> But fickle Fortune frowns on me,
> And I maun cross the raging sea;
> But while my crimson currents flow,
> I'll love my Highland Lassie, O.

On the banks of the Ayr, the poet and his Mary exchanged Bibles, swore eternal love and planned to marry. Alas, Mary died of malignant fever at Greenock, and their marriage was never to be. Burns said sadly of *Highland Mary*:

> Wi' mony a vow, and locked embrace,
>   Our parting was fu' tender;
> And pledging aft to meet again,
>   We tore oursels asunder:
> But Oh, fell Death's untimely frost,
>   That nipt my Flower sae early!
> Now green's the sod, and cauld's the clay,
>   That wraps my Highland Mary!

Doubts have been cast on the character of Mary and the seriousness of her love for the poet, but such unworthy carping is silenced by the depth of feeling of the touching poem *To Mary in Heaven*:

> Thou lingering Star with lessening ray
>   That lovest to greet the early morn,
> Again thou usherest in the day
>   My Mary from my Soul was torn —
> O Mary! dear, departed Shade!
>   Where is thy place of blissful rest?
> Seest thou thy Lover lowly laid?
>   Hearest thou the groans that rend his breast?

> That sacred hour can I forget,
>   Can I forget the hallowed grove,
> Where by the winding Ayr we met,
>   To live one day of Parting Love?
> Eternity can not efface
>   Those records dear of transports past;
> Thy image at our last embrace,
>   Ah, little thought we 'twas our last!

Ayr gurgling kissed his pebbled shore,
    O'erhung with wild-woods, thick'ning, green;
The fragrant birch, and hawthorn hoar,
    Twined, am'rous round the raptured scene:
The flowers sprang wanton to be prest,
    The birds sang love on ev'ry spray;
Till too, too soon the glowing west
    Proclaimed the speed of winged day.

Still o'er these scenes my mem'ry wakes,
    And fondly broods with miser-care;
Time but th'impression stronger makes,
    As streams their channels deeper wear:
My Mary, dear, departed Shade!
    Where is thy place of blissful rest!
Seest thou thy Lover lowly laid!
    Hearest thou the groans that rend his breast!

Such pathos bestows immortality on love-poetry of the highest quality.

Burns's sympathies extend to the world of nature, for in his world man is merely *primus inter pares* and has a strong and binding kinship to the natural world. With true humility and artless simplicity, Burns can address himself to the humblest creations of God and speak with fellow-feeling. The laughter and the love combine to produce lyric poetry unequalled elsewhere in poesie. What other poet would address a louse? What other poet would address a haggis? What other poet would address a mountain daisy he has just ploughed under?

Wee, modest, crimson-tipped flow'r,
Thou's met me in an evil hour;
For I maun crush amang the stoure
        Thy slender stem:
To spare thee now is past my pow'r,
        Thou bonie gem.

What other poet would address a mouse whose home he has destroyed with the ploughshare?

Wee, sleeket, cowran, tim'rous beastie,
O, what a panic's in thy breastie!

And what other poet would compare himself with that mouse and envy him, as Burns does?

> Still, thou art blest, compar'd wi' me!
> The present only toucheth thee:
> But, Och! I backward cast my e'e,
>   On prospects drear!
> An' forward, tho' I canna see,
>   I guess an' fear!

Such deep humanity, such gentle and kindly humour, such loving focus on the smallest detail show the secret of Robert Burns's universal appeal — his unique combination of laughter and love. His sympathies extend to the poverty-stricken, the afflicted, the weary, the lowly, the field mouse, the auld farmer's auld mare Maggie, the limping hare, Burns's own dying pet sheep Mailie, and help them to laugh and to love. Burns's love extends from a single lady, a single flower, a single little mouse to all animate nature, to all fellow men. Put such love together with the laughter, and you have the key, I think, to the twin riddle of Robert Burns; the *combination* of his two finest qualities explains why he, and no other, is Scotland's national poet, and explains why he, and no other, is also the world's universal poet of the human heart. The paradox is resolved; the enigma is the laughter of love.

12

O what a canty warld were it

But deep this truth impress'd my mind —
Thro' all his works abroad,
The heart benevolent and kind
The most resembles God.

Burns Bust by Patric Park

In his fine book *The Scottish Tradition in Literature*, Kurt Wittig begins his chapter on Burns by pointing out a problem that confronts all who propose the Immortal Memory: 'Scotland's national bard has been the subject of so much study, criticism, and eulogy that it hardly seems possible to shed new light on any single facet of his achievement.'[42] The attempt to say something new about a literary figure can lead to absurdity of the variety perpetrated by Goldman when he says of another Robin, Robin Hood, 'And his legend is included in Percy's *Reliques*, which, it's easy to forget, was used by Shakespeare as a source for many of his plays.'[43] I confess to being guilty of forgetting this while at the same time hoping to avoid incurring derision for my approach to Burns. Taking off Burns's masks of ploughman poet, drum-beating patriot, hard drinker and libidinous lover in order to penetrate to the laughter of love and the reasons for the universal appeal of the poetry could lead to distortion in that a man's masks are part and parcel of the complete personality and must be taken into account fully. Burns's personality, while multi-faceted, is of necessity all of a piece, and must be viewed as completely integrated; the whole man comes to poetry, not just certain of his nobler aspects.

In the case of Burns, the physical appearance was striking. James Currie offers a typical verbal description of the poet:

> Burns was nearly five feet ten inches in height, and of a form that indicated agility as well as strength. His well-raised forehead, shaded with black curling hair, indicated extensive capacity. His eyes were large, dark, full of ardour and intelligence. His face was well formed; and his countenance uncommonly interesting and expressive. His mode of dressing, which was often slovenly, and a certain fulness and bend in his shoulders, characteristic of his original profession, disguised in some degree the natural symmetry and elegance of his form. The external appearance of Burns was most strikingly indicative of the character of his mind.[44]

An attempt to establish a psychological profile of Burns should start with the representations of the poet which can be taken to be reasonably authentic. Best known is Alexander Nasmyth's bust portrait from life of 1787, commissioned by William Creech for the Edinburgh Editions and now in the Scottish National Portrait Gallery in the capital. For the first Edinburgh Edition an engraving was prepared from the Nasmyth bust portrait by J. Beugo, and Burns gave additional sittings in 1787 for the engraving. In 1827-28, for Lockhart's life of the poet, Nasmyth added his bust portrait to the full figure of Burns taken from a pencil sketch made on a visit to Roslin Castle in 1787; the result is also on view now in the Scottish National

Portrait Gallery. In Lady Stairs House Museum in Edinburgh may be seen another full-figure painting of Burns in W.B. Johnstone's 'Sibbald's Circulating Library' of 1786. To this may be added a third full-figure representation in the Charles Martin Hardie picture of the meeting of Burns and the young Walter Scott in Sciennes Hill House, Edinburgh, the home of Professor Adam Ferguson; the House is now part of a tenement at No. 7 Braid Place, off Causewayside, and Hardie's painting is on display in the Chambers Institute in Peebles. In the Scottish National Portrait Gallery are to be seen two further important head-and-shoulders depictions of the poet — Archibald Skirving's 'keel' or chalk-drawing (not from life, but based on the Nasmyth bust portrait) hailed by Scott as 'the only good portrait of Burns' and Alexander Reid's miniature water-colour on ivory painted in 1795 in Dumfries and praised by Burns himself as 'the most remarkable likeness of what I am at this moment that I ever think was taken of anybody.'

Contemplating these pictures of Burns, the observer cannot but be struck by the man's beauty. The constitutional cage is a good, capable, athletic, stallion physique, handsome and well-formed. The fine physique is not shown in any distortion, and there are absolutely no signs of the dissipations of the legend. On the evidence of Scott's verbal portrait of Burns, I suspect that in real life the poet was a little more of the somatotonia type than the pictures suggest, more rugged, more dynamic, more square-jawed; this, I think, is shown by Scott's preference for the most mature of the bust portraits, Skirving's keeli-vine drawing. Burns's muscular and vigorous physique is of Kretschmer's *athletic* variety:

> The male athletic type is recognized by the strong development of the skeleton, the musculature and also the skin . . . A middle-sized to tall man, with particularly wide projecting shoulders, a superb chest, a firm stomach, and a trunk which tapers in its lower region, so that the pelvis, and the magnificent legs, sometimes seem almost graceful compared with the size of the upper limbs and particularly the hypertrophied shoulders.[45]

Using the 0 - 7 rating system Sheldon propounds in his *Scale for Temperament,*[46] constitutional psychology would give Burns the ratings of 3 - 6 - 4 in Sheldon's three categories of viscerontia, somatotonia and cerebrotonia, bearing in mind that one has as evidence paintings rather than photographs of the usual type and that the body is clothed. 3 for endomorphy, 4 for ectomorphy and 6 for mesomorphy suggests at least that Burns is mainly of the mesomorphic type, with some emphasis on ectomorphy. Sheldon's mesomorphic component is defined as follows:

> A physique heavily developed in this component, and showing a decrement in both the other components, is hard and rectangular, with a predominance of bone and muscle. The mesomorphic body is strong, tough, resistant to injury, and generally equipped for strenuous and exacting physical demands. The athlete, adventurer, or professional soldier might best be endowed with this type of physique.[47]

The personality traits that go with such a physique include assertiveness, love of physical adventure, energetic behaviour, need and love of exercise, need to dominate, love of risk and chance, bold directness of manner, physical courage, unrestrained voice, overmaturity of appearance, assertiveness and aggression under alcohol, and orientation toward the goals and activities of youth.

Such a personality is prideful and given to dramatisation. This suggests that Burns's ploughman and patriotic masks are *conscious*, not neurotic poses. The patriotic posture is very mesomorphic, with its stirring call for action, while the ploughman pose is more ectomorphic, a more discerning pose of modesty aware of carrying genius with it. The alcoholic exhibitionism, the admiration for the jolly beggars in Poosie Nancy's establishment, the dashing off of extempore verses at the dinner-table are mesomorphic behavioural traits, of course. All of Burns's poses suggest that he was fully aware of his own genius, a genius all the pictures show in the eye, supporting Scott's description of the amazing power of Burns's gaze. John Syme, the poet's best friend in Dumfries, confirms Scott's use of the word 'glowed' in connection with Burns's eyes:

> The poet's expression varied perpetually, according to the idea that predominated in his mind; and it was beautiful to remark how well the play of the lips indicated the sentiment he was about to utter. His eyes and lips — the first remarkable for fire, and the second for flexibility — formed at all times an index to his mind . . . I cordially concur with what Sir Walter Scott says of the poet's eyes. In animated moments, and particularly when his dander was roused by instances of tergiversation, meanness, or tyranny, they were actually like coals of living fire.[48]

An uninhibited, unrestrained, uncontrolled reticular activating system is one of the characteristics of genius, and Burns's direct gaze suggests that he had good emotional contact with his own emotional centres which gave him his genius, his power to compose immortal poetry.

Here is Burns striking his pose in his introduction to his *Commonplace Book 1783-1785:*

> *Observations, Hints, Songs, Scraps of Poetry, &c. by Robert Burness*, a man who had little art in making money, and still less in keeping it; but was, however, a man of some sense, a great deal of honesty, and unbounded good-will to every creature, rational, or irrational. As he was but little indebted to a scholastic education, and bred at a plough-tail, his performances must be strongly tinctured with his unpolished rustic way of life; but as, I believe, they are really his own, it may be some entertainment to a curious observer of human nature to see how a ploughman thinks and feels, under the pressure of love, ambition, anxiety, grief, with the like cares and passions, which, however diversified by the modes and manners of life, operate pretty much alike, I believe, in all the species.

Behind the self-denigrating, conscious pose, Burns is aware of his ability to depict the universal.

The same pose is struck in the preface to the Kilmarnock Edition in which Burns nevertheless does not shrink from the word 'genius' in his self-assessment:

> Now that he appears in the public character of an author, he does it with fear and trembling. So dear is fame to the rhyming tribe, that even he, an obscure, nameless Bard, shrinks aghast at the thought of being branded as 'an impertinent blockhead, obtruding his nonsense on the world; and, because he can make a shift to jingle a few doggerel Scotch rhymes together, looking upon himself as a poet of no small consequence forsooth!'
>
> It is an observation of that celebrated poet, Shenstone, whose divine elegies do honour to our language, our nation, and our species, that '*Humility* has depressed many a genius to a hermit, but never raised one to fame!' If any critic catches at the word *genius*, the author tells him once for all, that he certainly looks upon himself as possest of some poetic abilities, otherwise his publishing in the manner he has done, would be a manoeuvre below the worst character, which he hopes his worst enemy will ever give him.

Beneath the self-deprecatory rhetoric lie Burns's clearly-stated awareness of his genius and his desire that it be recognized. The poses, the masks fall firmly into place; the setting of the stone is being made plainer in order to make the stone shine brighter. Compensation has a role to play in Burns's motives for writing poetry. For instance, the first thing one finds him telling John Moore is that he is of lowly birth (Mauchline, August 2nd, 1787):

> I have not the most distant pretensions to assume that character which the pye-coated guardians of escutcheons call a Gentleman . . . Gules, Purpure, Argent, &c. quite disowned me. . . . I was born a very poor man's son.

Seeking to right the balance, Burns seeks compensation in dissipation, in literary exhibitionism at supper tables, and in the ploughman pose he maintained in the Edinburgh salons, taking delight in hammering across rich carpets on his ploughman shanks. Yet the core attitudes and thoughts in his poetry reflect as his aim ultimate simplicity in life; the laughter of love leads him to value above all else such qualities as honesty, authenticity, integrity, worth, pride, dignity, independence. Burns in the end settles for less than do those of high lineage in physical and financial terms, but settles for so much more than others know in emotional and spiritual terms. The frills and spurious pleasures of society are ultimately rejected in favour of man's own worth. Here Burns has much in common with Cicero's *De Senectute* or Horace's desire to retire to his Sabine farm, working under simple, hard conditions leading to worth, pride, honesty. Here is the second version of the poem *Written in Friar's Carse Hermitage, on Nith-Side:*

> Life is but a day at most,
> Sprung from night, in darkness lost;
> Hope not sunshine every hour,
> Fear not clouds will always lour.
> Happiness is but a name,
> Make Content and Ease thy aim.
> Ambition is a meteor gleam,
> Fame a restless, airy dream;
> Pleasures, insects on the wing
> Round Peace, the tenderest flower of spring;
> Those that sip the dew alone,
> Make the butterflies thy own;
> Those that would the bloom devour,

Crush the locusts, save the flower.
For the Future be prepar'd,
Guard, wherever thou canst guard,
But thy utmost duly done,
Welcome what thou canst not shun:
Follies past, give thou to air;
Make their consequence thy care:
Keep the name of Man in mind,
And dishonour not thy kind.

Such recognition of man's ultimate worth, such basic honesty is the noblest motive of life, but usually too difficult for most to attain. Aiming at this lofty goal is important for Burns in finding inspiration. Failing in his own estimation to live up to the high ideal he has set himself leads him to throw himself passionately into the world, seeking praise or the consolation of the bottle; in failing, he suffers, and this reactivates pride, spurs him to attempt once more to be authentic and inspires him to seek true worth once again in life and in poetry. Such a cyclic view of Burns's inspiration explains the apparent contradictions in the biography and the legend, and also would explain why his later poetry does not match the quality of his Coila-inspired verse in that Burns did not fail enough in his later life to be as nobly inspired in reaction.

True honesty is a goal few, if any, can attain. One is reminded of the cynic philosopher Diogenes walking around in broad daylight with a lighted lantern, searching for an honest man. But this does not diminish the honesty itself; on the contrary, the value of the goal is enhanced by its not being attained. Burns here is one with Browning and his robust optimism which led him to say in effect that one may aim for ten and succeed in that goal but would do so much better to aim for a thousand and partly miss the mark. The goal is not diminished by its not being attained. Hence, I think, derives the universal appeal of Robert Burns, who urges mankind to value the ideal it *can* hold despite the failings of the weak flesh. If the spirit values honesty, authenticity, integrity, worth, pride, dignity, independence, that is what matters; such is the highest possible honour-value in this fallen world.

O what a canty warld were it,
Would pain and care, and sickness spare it;
And fortune favor worth and merit,
    As they deserve.

The *Poem on Life* of 1796 tells Colonel de Payster, and all mankind, that the world is indeed a fallen one in which Burns's values do not find their fulfillment. Such also is the message given Andrew Aiken in Burns's *Epistle to a Young Friend:*

> Ye'll try the world soon my lad,
>   And Andrew dear believe me,
> Ye'll find mankind an unco squad,
>   And muckle they may grieve ye:
> For care and trouble set your thought,
>   Ev'n when your end's attained;
> And a' your views may come to nought,
>   Where ev'ry nerve is strained.
>
> I'll no say, men are villains a';
>   The real, harden'd wicked,
> Wha hae nae check but human law,
>   Are to a few restricked
> But Och, mankind are unco weak,
>   An' little to be trusted;
> If Self the wavering balance shake,
>   It's rarely right adjusted!

It is to attempt the right adjustment of the balance that Burns writes his poetry. In his *Second Epistle to Lapraik*, he tells his brother bard 'Ne'er mind how Fortune waft an' warp: She's but a bitch' and advises him to write at the very moment his Muse tires of the world:

> Her dowf excuses pat me mad;
> 'Conscience,' says I, 'ye thowless jad!
> 'I'll write, an' that a hearty blaud,
>   'This vera night;
> 'So dinna ye affront your trade,
>   'But rhyme it right.'

The *Third Epistle to Lapraik* shows Burns falling into bad company, bad whisky and bad verse yet finding therein release and motivation:

> But let the kirk-folk ring their bells,
> Let's sing about our noble sels;
> We'll cry nae jads frae heathen hills

> To help, or roose us,
> But browster wives an' whiskie stills,
> They are the muses.

And Burns tells Moore about the regenerative effect of writing (Mauchline, August 2nd, 1787):

> My passions, when once lighted up, raged like so many devils, till they got vent in rhyme; and then the conning over my verses, like a spell, soothed all into quiet!

Honesty comes quickly upon the conclusion of the poems, for the laughter of love is restored to its central place in the scheme of things and humorous self-appraisal is reasserted. Here, for instance, is the close of the *Third Epistle to Lapraik*:

> Then I maun rin amang the rest
>   An' quat my chanter;
> Sae I subscribe mysel in haste,
>   Yours, RAB THE RANTER.

And honesty and restored laughter go together in the conclusion of the *Letter to James Tait, of Glenconner*:

> Assist poor Simson a' ye can,
> Ye'll fin' him just an honest man:
> Sae I conclude and quat my chanter,
> Yours, saint or sinner,
>   RAB THE RANTER.

All these threads of thought come together in the *Elegy on the Death of Robert Ruisseaux*, the companion piece to the birth poem *Rantin' Rovin' Robin*. 'Ruisseaux' is the poet's name in French, so this *Elegy* is intended to match the birth poem and appraise the career of the lad born in Kyle:

> Now Robin lies in his last lair,
> He'll gabble rhyme, nor sing nae mair,
> Cauld poverty, wi' hungry stare,
>   Nae mair shall fear him;
> Nor anxious fear, nor cankert care
>   E'er mair come near him.

> To tell the truth, they seldom fash't him,
> Except the moment that they crush't him;
> For sune as chance or fate had hush't 'em
>   Tho' e'er sae short,
> Then wi' a rhyme or song he lash't 'em,
>   And thought it sport.
>
> Tho' he was bred to kintra wark,
> And counted was baith wight and stark,
> Yet that was never Robin's mark
>   To mak a man;
> But tell him he was learn'd and clark,
>   Ye roos'd him then!

The laughter of love finds its expression in poetry which then provides an answer to the failings of the universe, emphasizing the worth of the individual and, through humour, restoring the universal balance.

The universal creed is sublimely simple and profoundly comforting — 'A man's a man for a' that' is the answer to all oppression, every care, heart-breaking sorrow and back-breaking poverty. The laughter of love throws this message in the teeth of adversity and asserts the essential dignity and worth of mortal existence. With this creed no right-thinking man can quarrel; to the tune of this creed all free nations must march; in this creed rich and poor, happy and miserable, young and old find their only justification on earth; this creed alone must be the basis of individual, national and international honour. If men remember this together every January 25th, it were, indeed, a canty world.

> 'To give my counsels all in one,
> 'Thy tuneful flame still careful fan;
> 'Preserve the dignity of Man,
>   'With Soul erect;
> 'And trust, the Universal Plan
>   'Will all protect.'

This is the climactic injunction of Coila in *The Vision*, and this highest of all themes informs Burns's poetry from first to last. The theme lives in the primal vision of the Muse and persists undiminished to the *Poetical Inscription for an Altar to Independence* of 1795, the year before the poet's death:

Thou, of an independent mind
With soul resolv'd, with soul resigned;
Prepar'd pow'r's proudest frown to brave,
Who wilt not be, nor have a slave;
Virtue alone who dost revere,
Thy own reproach alone dost fear,
Approach this shrine, and worship here.

And at the very core of Burns's poetical creed as expounded in the *Epistle to Davie* are found in close juxtaposition emphasis on the holiness of the heart's affections above all other measures of human happiness and emphasis on the laughter of love:

It's no in titles nor in rank
It's no in wealth like Lon'on Bank,
  To purchase peace and rest;
It's no in makin muckle, mair:
It's no in books; it's no in Lear,
  To make us truly blest:
If Happiness hae not her seat
And center in the breast,
We may be wise, or rich, or great,
  But never can be blest:
      Nae treasures, nor pleasures
        Could make us happy lang;
      The heart ay's the part ay,
        That makes us right or wrang. . .

All hail! ye tender feelings dear!
The smile of love, the friendly tear,
  The sympathetic glow!
Long since, this world's thorny ways
Had number'd out my weary days,
  Had it not been for you!
Fate still has blest me with a friend
  In ev'ry care and ill;
And oft a more endearing band,
  A tye more tender still.
      It lightens, it brightens,
        The tenebrific scene,
      To meet with, and greet with,
        My Davie or my Jean!

This is the highest message that the laughter of love has to teach us — the infinite worth of the individual human soul. The lillies of the field, each sparrow that falls, the very hairs on our heads are counted by the laughter of love, hence poetry finds its most poignant images in the wounded hare, the crimson-tipped mountain daisy, the cowering and terrified mouse, the spring rose but yet in the bud. The universe comes alive for us only when we learn to listen to the laughter of love, and life has meaning for us only when we learn to set infinite value on our fellow human being. The laughter of love alone can mend the broken heart and wipe away all tears.

Burns's letters reinforce the message of the poetry, putting the stress firmly where it always must be, on honesty, integrity, love. He writes to Robert Muir (Mossgiel, March 7th, 1788):

> But an honest man has nothing to fear . . . even granting that he may have been the sport, at times, of passions and instincts; he goes to a great unknown Being who could have no other end in giving him existence but to make him happy; who gave him those passions and instincts, and well knows their force.

His self-assessment expressed to John Erskine, Earl of Mar, shows steady focus on family and freedom, on love (Dumfries, April 13th, 1793):

> Burns was a poor man, from birth; & an Exciseman, by necessity: but — I will say it! — the sterling of his honest worth, no poverty could debase; & his independant British mind, Oppression might bend, but could not subdue! — Have not I, to me, a more precious stake in my Country's welfare than the richest Dukedom in it? — I have a large family of children, & the probability of more . . .

And the essence of his philosophy is perfectly caught when he can state his creed thus simply:[49]

> Whatever mitigates the woes, or increases the happiness of others, this is my criterion of goodness; and whatever injures society at large, or any individual in it, this is my measure of iniquity.
> God knows I am no saint; I have a whole host of follies and sins to answer for; but if I could, and I believe I do it as far as I can, I would wipe away all tears from all eyes.

The spae-wife's prophecy has come true; the heart has always come first:

> He'll hae misfortunes great and sma',
> but ay a heart aboon them a';
> He'll be a credit till us a',
>   We'll a' be proud o' Robin.

The laughter of love persists to the end, unto death and through death. About to die in great misery, Burns can ask Mrs. Maria Riddell at Brow Well, three weeks before his death, 'Well, Madam, have you any commands for the other world?' And the beadsman of Nithside can assert in the poem *Written in Friar's Carse Hermitage* that the laughter of love does indeed persist to the other side of the veil; if it cannot, then nothing can:

> Thus, resigned and quiet, creep
> To thy bed of lasting sleep:
> Sleep, whence thou shalt ne'er awake,
> Night, where dawn shall never break,
> Till Future Life, future no more,
> To light and joy the Good restore,
> To light and joy unknown before.

Robert Burns was tragically short-lived, being granted only 37 years in a universe which did not see fit to be nice wi' Robin but chose to inflict upon him a hard, savage and almost brutal existence in a land not noted for the salubrity of its climate. As Robertson Nicoll put it in *The British Weekly* (January 16, 1902):

In the first place, the Scotsman is a son of the rock. The circumstances of his birth and upbringing are as a rule very stern. He is cradled in the storm; he has to fight for life in a rough climate, in a huddle of grey houses. The amenities of life are by no means plentiful. As a rule money is scarce. There are few demonstrations of affection; one is made to feel that he must trust himself, that man is a soldier, and life is a fight.

This is certainly how life found Burns, as can be seen when one traces his hardships from the deprivations of childhood through the attempts to till the unfriendly soil of Mossgiel, the frantic decision to emigrate to Jamaica, the gruelling work in all weathers as exciseman to the pathetic deathbed. Matthew Arnold has pointed out that from such an environment one would not *a priori* expect beautiful poetry:

> The real Burns is of course in his Scotch poems . . . But this world
> of Scotch drink, Scotch religion, and Scotch manners is against a
> poet, not for him, when it is not a partial countryman who reads
> him; for in itself it is not a beautiful world, and no one can deny
> that it is of advantage to a poet to deal with a beautiful world.

On January 25, 227 years ago, a blast o' Januar wind blew
hansel in on Rantin', Rovin' Robin, the lad new-born in Kyle to the
blessing and the curse of the gift of song. From the barren soil of
Mossgiel there sprang a singer for his brief moments in that cold
northern sun, and sing he did — songs of love and of lust, songs of
sainthood and of sin, songs of drink and of despair, songs of humour
and of satire, songs of pathos and of bathos, songs of liberty and of
independence, songs of pride and of worth. Many of the songs were
bad, some of the songs were good, and a surprising number of them
were and are great. We must needs accept that in that abundant
lyrical outpouring much of what was produced was dross, but it is in
dross that diamonds are to be found, polished and cherished by the
generations. The song did not, could not last, but those tragically few,
glorious years have left us a legacy of verse without which the whole
world would be the poorer. If Sir Walter Scott gave Scotland back
her history, Robert Burns gave all men a new idea of themselves as
he sang of human nature, with its strengths and its failings, its dignity,
its liberty. Above all, Burns was born, as the spae-wife said over his
infant cradle, to be the great poet of the human heart, and the great
poet of the human heart wrote with a sublime simplicity of the beni-
son of which the humblest may so freely partake:

> Gie me ae spark o' Nature's fire,
> That's a' the learning I desire;
> Then tho' I drudge thro' dub an' mire
>   At pleugh or cart,
> My Muse, tho' hamely in attire,
>   May touch the heart.

Burns tells us in the Dedication to the Edinburgh Edition of
1787 precisely where Coila found him:

> The poetic genius of my country found me, as the prophetic bard
> Elijah did Elisha — at the PLOUGH; and threw her inspiring
> mantle over me. She bade me sing the loves, the joys, the rural
> scenes and rural pleasures of my native soil, in my native tongue:
> I tuned my wild, artless notes as she inspired.

It sometimes seems that Burns is not one man but rather a mos-
aic of lovable poses: if you want a great drinker, he'll strike that pose,
if you want the great lover, he'll accommodate you. If you want him
to follow a rustic model, he'll write from Ellisland as the Nithsdale
Horace; if you want the Miltonic Satan to be his model, that too, can
be arranged. And the poseur is profligate of his health and spendthrift
of his abilities, prey at once to sudden passions and deep depressions,
until an unpleasant and untimely death puts an end to the singer and
his imperfections. Yet amid the toils and the troubles can be discerned
a transcendant magnificence of spirit which deserves to be honoured
by posterity, as Thomas Carlyle gruffly asserts in *The Edinburgh
Review* (1828):

> Granted, the ship comes into harbour with shrouds and tackle
> damaged; the pilot is blameworthy; he has not been all-wise and
> all-powerful, but to know *how* blameworthy, tell us first whether
> his voyage has been round the globe, or only to Ramsgate and the
> Isle of Dogs.

When we cut through the criticism, the legends and the poses, we find
the essential Robert Burns, the poet of love and of liberty:

> Flow gently, sweet Afton, among thy green braes,
> Flow gently, I'll sing thee a song in thy praise;
> My Mary's asleep by thy murmuring stream,
> Flow gently, sweet Afton, disturb not her dream.

The poet who charges the gently-flowing Afton Water not to disturb
his sleeping Highland Mary is no ordinary love-poet, for the poise of
the poem and the poet's control are exquisite. And for such love to be
able to exist, mankind's spirit must be free. As Andrew Fletcher of
Saltoun said in 1698, 'Allow me to make the songs of a country, and
I will allow you to make its laws.' It was Robert Burns who made the
songs of Scotland, finding the vital need for love and for liberty in
public and in private life alike. As he tells Dr. Blacklock:

> To make a happy fire-side clime
> 　　　To weans and wife,
> That's the true Pathos and Sublime
> 　　　Of Human life.

Or as he puts it in *The Cotter's Saturday Night*:

> From scenes like these, old Scotia's grandeur springs,
>   That makes her lov'd at home, rever'd abroad:
> Princes and lords are but the breath of kings,
>   'An honest man's the noble work of God.'

Robert Burns goes far beyond the boundaries of Scotland and her tongue to sing of the brotherhood of *all* men and of the great universal poles of human life — love and liberty. At the beginning of the *AEneid*, Virgil tells us, *Sunt lacrimae rerum et mentem mortalis tangunt*, 'Human deeds have their tears, and mortality touches the heart.' The finest of Burns's poems have precisely this quality of bringing the tears to the universal eye, of taking us all right into the *lacrimae rerum*.

And when Burns preaches the brotherhood of man, he does so in the unspoken context of the fatherhood of an higher power he sought often to suppress or deny. Writing from Ellisland, Tuesday, February 16th, 1790, he ended his letter as follows:

> Finally, Brethren, farewell! Whatsoever things are lovely,
> whatsoever things are gentle, whatsoever things are charitable,
> whatsoever things are kind, think on these things, and think on
>
>   ROBᵀ BURNS.

Quaecumque vera, quaecumque pudica, quaecumque justa, quaecumque sancta, quaecumque amabilia' . . . the message of St Paul's letter to the Philippians, the motto of the University of Alberta, Burns's closing words to us all.

In the centennial year, 1859, Ralph Waldo Emerson proposed the health to the Immortal Memory before the Boston Burns Club and summed up as follows:

> The people who care nothing for literature and poetry care for Burns . . . He has given voice to all the experiences of common life; he has endeared the farmhouse and cottage, patches and poverty, beans and barley; ale, the poor man's wine; hardship, the fear

of debt, the dear society of weans and wife, of brothers and sisters, proud of each other, knowing so few and finding amends for want and obscurity in books and thought . . . The memory of Burns — every man's and boy's and girl's head carries snatches of his songs, and can say them by heart, and what is strangest of all, never learned them from a book, but from mouth to mouth. The wind whispers them, the birds whistle them, the corn, barley, and bulrushes hoarsely rustle them; nay the music boxes are framed and toothed to play them; the hand organs of the Savoyards in all cities repeat them; and the chimes of bells ring them in the spires. They are the property and the solace of mankind.

To sum up on Robert Burns is a heavy task for which I lack the necessary degree of presumption. Fortunately, posterity has already taken Burns to its embrace, and his international reputation needs no words of mine to enhance it further. Neither psychologist nor literary critic can explain the phenomenon of Burns, and the humblest heart that is privy to the laughter of love finds no need of explanation. We simply note with gratitude the lyrical outpourings of a full heart which have captured for all men, all nations, all time the essence of our common humanity. The life was short and brutal, its start violent and its ending pathetic, but for a few, Heaven-sent years the poet shared with mankind his God-given gift of song. Those whom the powers of the universe love are not with us long, be they saints or sinners, and while they are with us we fail to cherish them or understand them, leaving them to die wretchedly. As Burns told his physician, Dr. Maxwell, 'What business has a physician to waste his time on me? I am a poor pigeon, not worth plucking. Alas! I have not feathers enough upon me to carry me to my grave.' We can, however, pay compensation to the memory of such men by accepting the miracle of their inspiration and hearkening with our hearts to their visionary insights into eternal truths. If we practice the laughter of love, we do honour to the Immortal Memory of Robert Burns.

Speaking in Glasgow on the centenary of Burns's death on July 21st, 1896, Lord Rosebery with simple but moving eloquence captured the essence of the miracle called Burns in a single paragraph it were impossible to better:

> Try to reconstruct Burns as he was. A peasant, born in a cottage that no sanitary inspector in these days would tolerate for a moment; struggling with desperate effort against pauperism, almost in vain; snatching at scraps of learning in the intervals of toil, as it were with his teeth; a heavy silent lad, proud of his ploughing. All

of a sudden, without preface or warning, he breaks out into exquisite song, like a nightingale from the brushwood, and continues singing as sweetly — with nightingale pauses — till he dies. A nightingale sings because he cannot help it; he can only sing exquisitely, because he knows no other. So it was with Burns. What is this but inspiration? One can no more measure or reason about it than measure or reason about Niagara.[50]

We cannot understand, we cannot analyse the phenomenon of Burns's greatness any more than could those who lined the streets that day one hundred years earlier when the coffin carrying the poet's exhausted body wended its melancholy way from Mill Vennel to St. Michael's Churchyard. The mortal remains of the poet went from the penniless misery of his last home to a public funeral he would have hated, the awkward squad firing over his coffin the volleys he feared they would, his wife labouring to give birth to his posthumous child. The interment in a pauper's grave in a corner of the graveyard must surely have served to underline mankind's unfortunate treatment of its poets. Yet not the slightest hint of bitterness disfigures the perfect poise, the calm serenity of the prophetic *A Bard's Epitaph*, one of the finest labours of the laughter of love which in its frank and peaceful self-assessment stills all criticism:

> Is there a whim-inspir'd fool,
> Owre fast for thought, owre hot for rule,
> Owre blate to seek, owre proud to snool,
>   Let him draw near;
> And o'er this grassy heap sing dool,
>   And drap a tear.

> Is there a Bard of rustic song,
> Who, noteless, steals the crouds among
> That weekly this area throng,
>   Oh, pass not by!
> But, with a frater-feeling strong,
>   Here, heave a sigh.

> Is there a man whose judgment clear,
> Can others teach the course to steer,
> Yet runs, himself, life's mad career,
>   Wild as the wave,
> Here pause — and, thro' the starting tear,
>   Survey this grave.

The poor Inhabitant below
Was quick to learn and wise to know,
And keenly felt the friendly glow,
     And softer flame;
But thoughtless follies laid him low,
     And stain'd his name!

Reader attend — whether thy soul
Soars fancy's flights beyond the pole,
Or darkling grubs this earthly hole,
     In low pursuit,
Know, prudent, cautious, self-controul
     Is Wisdom's root.

This was neither saint nor sinner; this was a man, a man living more intensely than most our common life on earth, but still a man, human, fallible, imperfect. In his universal imperfection subsists his universal poetic appeal, as Lord Rosebery told his Glasgow audience in 1896:

Mankind is helped in its progress almost as much by the study of imperfection as by the contemplation of perfection. Had we nothing before us in our futile and halting lives but saints and the ideal, we might well fail altogether. . . . Man, after all, is not ripened by virtue alone. Were it so, this world were a paradise of angels. No! Like the growth of the earth, he is the fruit of all the seasons — the accident of a thousand accidents, a living mystery, moving through the seen to the unseen. He is sown in dishonour; he is matured under all the varieties of heat and cold — in mist and wrath, in snow and vapours, in the melancholy of autumn, in the torpor of winter, as well as in the rapture and fragrance of summer, or the balmy affluence of the spring — its breath, its sunshine, its dew. And at the end he is reaped — the product, not of one climate, but of all; not of good alone, but of evil; not of joy alone, but of sorrow — perhaps mellowed and ripened, perhaps stricken and withered and sour. How, then, shall we judge any one? How, at any rate, shall we judge a giant, great in gifts and great in temptation, great in strength and great in weakness? Let us glory in his strength and be comforted in his weakness. And when we thank Heaven for the inestimable gift of Burns, we do not need to remember wherein he was imperfect, we cannot bring ourselves to regret that he was made of the same clay as ourselves.[51]

Perfection lies outwith the realm of human possibility, but laughter and love do not. When the imperfection of life oppresses us, when the best-laid schemes of mice and men gang agley and we are left with nought but grief and pain, Burns helps us to laugh and to love. In the universality of his creed we may identify ourselves, our hopes and our fears, and we discover an essential harmony at the core of the world's discord and clamour. The laughter of love can, nay *must* be the basis on which a better life can be built, both individually and collectively. Individually, Burns's creed goes beyond the bonds of the usual concept of human relationship to elevate and ennoble the love of man for woman, for nature in all her tenderest aspects, for fellow man. Collectively, Burns's creed goes beyond mere politics to sing the universal charter of mankind's self-respect, mankind's right to warmth, worth, dignity and independence:

> Is there, for honest Poverty
>   That hangs his head, and a' that;
> The coward-slave, we pass him by,
>   We dare be poor for a' that!
>   For a' that, and a' that,
>   Our toils obscure, and a' that,
>   The rank is but the guinea's stamp,
>   The Man's the gowd for a' that.
>
> What though on hamely fare we dine,
>   Wear hoddin grey, and a' that.
> Gie fools their silks, and knaves their wine,
>   A Man's a Man for a' that.
>   For a' that, and a' that,
>   Their tinsel show, and a' that;
>   The honest man, though e'er sae poor,
>   Is king o' men for a' that.
>
> Ye see yon birkie ca'd, a lord,
>   What struts, and stares, and a' that,
> Though hundreds worship at his word,
>   He's but a coof for a' that.
>   For a' that, and a' that.
>   His ribband, star and a' that,
>   The man of independant mind,
>   He looks and laughs at a' that.

A prince can mak a belted knight,
  A marquis, duke, and a' that;
But an honest man's aboon his might,
  Gude faith he mauna fa' that!
    For a' that, and a' that,
      Their dignities, and a' that,
    The pith o' Sense, and pride o' Worth,
      Are higher rank than a' that.

Then let us pray that come it may,
  As come it will for a' that,
That Sense and Worth, o'er a' the earth
  May bear the gree, and a' that.
    For a' that, and a' that,
      Its coming yet for a' that,
    That Man to Man the warld o'er,
      Shall brothers be for a' that.

'Alle Menschen werden Bröder' — this is the theme of Schiller's *Ode to Joy*, this is the theme of the Ninth Symphony, this is the message of Rousseau. But how *simply* it is expressed by the Scottish bard. It is fitting that Henry Bain Smith's statue of Burns in my native Aberdeen does not depict the poet of the laughter of love wearing a cincture of Delphic bay or holding impressive-looking scrolls; rather, it depicts the poet bareheaded, ploughman's plaid over his shoulder, his right hand holding his guid Scots bonnet and his left holding a daisy, the most appropriate symbol one could devise for such a simple, sublime poet.

This is the real Burns, this is Scotland's national poet, her *national* poet because he could express so sublimely what is *universal*. Such a poet is a poet for all seasons, all countries, all times. He is not only a nationalist poet, he is not only a Scottish poet, he is not only a love poet — he is a *universal* poet. This is the poet of whom Burns Night orators talk each year as they propose the toast to the Immortal Memory and invite their company to join in the singing of *Auld Lang Syne*. This song is sung all over the world by people of many races, many colours, many tongues, many creeds, so it must express sentiments that are universally shared, yet its expression remains unforgettably Scottish. This is the secret of Burns's unique appeal; this is the laughter of love:

Should auld acquaintance be forgot
And never brought to mind?
Should auld acquaintance be forgot,
And days o' lang syne?

And surely ye'll be your pint stowp!
And surely I'll be mine!
And we'll tak a cup o' kindness yet
For auld lang syne.

We twa hae run about the braes,
And pou'd the gowans fine;
But we've wander'd mony a weary fitt,
Sin auld lang syne.

We twa hae paidl'd in the burn,
Frae morning sun till dine;
But seas between us braid hae roar'd
Sin auld lang syne.

And there's a hand, my trusty fiere!
And gie's a hand o' thine!
And we'll tak a right gude-willie-waught,
For auld lang syne.

For auld lang syne, my dear,
For auld lang syne,
We'll tak a cup o' kindness yet,
For auld lang syne.

On January 25th each year we drink a toast to the Immortal Memory of the poet of the laughter of love and for one brief, shining moment we are one with our dear ones, one with our fellow men and women, one with the little mouse with whom we share a common destiny and mortality. We lift our eyes to the hills and say with the old farmer, 'Aye, Rabbie Burns was the boy!'

Ellisland, Tuesday, February 16th, 1790.

Finally, Brethren, farewell! Whatsoever things are lovely, whatsoever things are gentle, whatsoever things are charitable, whatsoever things are kind, think on these things, and think on

ROBERT BURNS.

Notes

Since it seems desirable in a work as modest in scope as the present one to keep footnoting to a minimum, I have not quoted chapter and verse on every passage of verse or prose cited. Extracts from Burns's poems are based on the 1968 three-volume Oxford edition edited by James Kinsley, unless otherwise noted. Extracts from prose writings by or about Burns have been taken from the 1806 edition of James Currie's *Works* and from J. De Lancey Ferguson's 1931 edition of the *Letters*, unless otherwise noted. It has, of course, proven impossible to find the original sources of all the age-old jokes adapted and retold throughout the present work; the bibliography offers details of such useful collections as those of Burnett, the Elliots, Macgregor and McPhee.

[1]*Punch on Scotland*, ed. Miles Kington (London, 1977), p. 137.

[2]Matthew Arnold, 'The Study of Poetry', *Essays in Criticism*, Second Series, in *The English Poets*, ed. T.H. Ward (1880).

[3]Alistair MacLean, 'Introducing Scotland', *Alistair MacLean Introduces Scotland*, ed. Alastair M. Dunnett (New York, 1972), pp. 14-15.

[4]Hugh MacDiarmid, *Burns Today and Tomorrow* (Edinburgh, 1959), pp. 1,2.

[5]John Barclay Burns, in *The Presbyterian Record* (November, 1979), p. 29.

[6]*The Selected Poems of Robert Burns*, ed. David Daiches (Bungay, Suffolk, 1979), p. 20.

[7]M. Fabius Quintilian, *Institutio Oratoria* XII. 5,4, quoted from *The Institutio Oratoria of Quintilian*, trans. H.E. Butler, 4 vols. (London, 1922), IV, p. 411.

[8]David Daiches, *Robert Burns* (New York, 1952), p. 5.

[9]On the rumoured descent of Burns from a Gaelic bard named Campbell, see D. MacDonald, 'The Bard and the Campbell Link', *Scottish Field* (January, 1979), pp. 12-13.

[10]The earliest foundations of Burns Clubs were those in Greenock (1801), Paisley (1805), Kilmarnock (1808) and Dunfermline (1812).

[11]Richard Gordon, 'Have another dram', *The Financial Post Magazine* (September, 1976), p. 5.

[12]Patrick Ryan, 'Grand Tour of the Greater Scottish Delusions' *Punch on Scotland*, p. 34.

[13]*The Autobiography of John Galt*, 2 vols. (London, 1833), II, pp. 280-1.

[14]Nicholas Fairbairn of Fordell, 'The Law of Scotland', *Alistair MacLean Introduces Scotland*, pp. 189-90.

[15]Forbes Macgregor, *Macgregor's Mixture* (Edinburgh, 1976, 1981), p. 111. A full account of Burns's phrenological development is to be found in *The Life of Robert Burns*, ed. James Currie, rev. Robert Chambers (Edinburgh, 1838), pp. 75-6.

[16]See, for instance, *The Scottish Tradition in Canada*, ed. W. Stanford Reid, in The History of Canada's People series published by McClelland and Stewart for the Dept. of the Secretary of State of Canada. See also *Some Scots: Shaping Canada*, ed. J.A. McIntyre and Elizabeth Waterson For the Canadian Association for Scottish Studies, vols. IX-X, 1981-2. Donaldson, Gordon, *The Scots Overseas,* London, Hale, 1966.

[17]*Anglo-Saxon Poetry*, trans. R.K. Gordon (London, 1926, 1959), p. 303.

[18]Justin Isherwood, 'A Pitch for a Midwinter Holiday', *The Milwaukee Journal* (January 25th, 1981), p. 14.

[19]Henry Mackenzie in *The Lounger* (December 9th, 1786), repr. in *Robert Burns: The Critical Heritage* ed. Donald A. Low (London, 1974), p. 70.

[20]Sir Walter Scott, reminiscence printed by Lockhart, *Life of Scott*, (1857), vol. I, repr. in *Burns As Others Saw Him*, ed. W.L. Renwick (Edinburgh, 1959), pp. 24-5.

[21]Henry Mackenzie, as quoted in Harold W. Thomson, *Anecdotes and Egotism of H.M.* (1927), repr. in *Burns As Others Saw Him*, p. 3.

[22]J.A. Carruth, *Robert Burns Scotland* (Norwich, 1971), p. 7.

[23]David Sillar, as quoted in Josiah Walker, *Life of Burns* (1811), repr. in *Burns As Others Saw Him*, pp. 2-3.

[24]Sir Walter Scott, reminiscence printed by Lockhart, *Life of Scott* (1857), vol. I, repr. in *Burns As Others Saw Him*, pp. 22-3.

[25]*Doric Spice*, ed. Forbes Macgregor (Edinburgh, 1956, 1960), p. 45.

[26]John Moore, 'An Englishman looks at Burns', *Scotland's Magazine* (January, 1959), p. 54.

[27]Hugh Douglas, *Robert Burns — A Life* (Newton Abbot, 1977), p. 12.

[28]Maria Riddell, 'Some Account of Robert Burns', *The Edinburgh Magazine or Literary Miscellany* (September, 1796), pp. 172-3.

[29]Sir Walter Scott, as quoted in *Burns As Others Saw Him*, p. 25.

[30]*William Dunbar — Poems*, ed. James Kinsley (Oxford, 1958), p. 75.

[31]'Two Discourses Concerning the Affairs of Scotland' (Edinburgh, 1698), in *Andrew Fletcher of Saltoun — Selected Political Writings and Speeches*, ed. David Daiches (Edinburgh, 1979), p. 28.

[32]From the 'Albion' edition, p. 146.

[33]These stanzas were first published in the Hogg and Motherwell edition, and the present text is from the 'Albion' edition. The stanzas are considered doubtful by some editors.

[34]Douglas Phillips-Birt, *A History of Seamanship* (London, 1971), p. 261, records that 'The most famous voyages of the tea clippers on the China route produced average speeds of a fraction under 6 1/2 knots. When on the Australian wool trade the *Cutty Sark* made a voyage at an average speed of 8 knots, but on this route respectable average speeds were just over 6 knots. It was then in the eighties of the last century.' The *Cutty Sark* Preservation Society (president, H.R.H. the Duke of Edinburgh) maintains the lovely old clipper on public view at Greenwich. Built in 1869 with a figurehead depicting Nannie, the reconditioned vessel now has a figurehead more decorously attired.

[35]*Doric Spice*, p. 60.

[36]James A. Guthrie, *A Corner of Carrick* (Newton Stewart, 1979), pp. 60-61.

[37]Arthur Michael Ramsey, *Introducing the Christian Faith* (London, 1961, 1970), p. 95.

[38]Quoted by Spider Robinson, 'The Reference Library', *Analog* CI, no. 12 (November 9th, 1981), p. 113n.

[39]Letters to Thomson (September, 1793) and Mrs. Dunlop (Ellisland, December 17th, 1788).

[40]Text from the 'Centenary Edition' IV, 69; described as 'improbable'.

[41]Text from the 'Albion' edition, p. 491.

[42]Kurt Wittig, *The Scottish Tradition in Literature* (Edinburgh, 1958), p. 199.

[43]James Goldman, *Robin and Marian* (New York, 1976), p. 31.

[44]*The Works of Robert Burns*, ed. James Currie, 4 vols., 5th ed. (London, 1806), I, pp. 230-31.

[45]Ernst Kretschmer, *Physique and Character* (New York, 1925), p. 24, quoted in Gardner Lindsey and Calvin S. Hall, *Theories of Personality* (New York, 1957, 1978), p. 341.

[46]W.H. Sheldon, *The Varieties of Temperament: A Psychology of Constitutional Differences* (New York, 1942), p. 26, quoted in *Theories of Personality*, p. 358.

[47]*Theories of Personality*, p. 347.

[48]From Hugh Douglas, *Robert Burns — a Life* (Newton Abbot, 1977), pp. 179-80.

[49]Letters to Mrs. Dunlop (Ellisland, June 21st, 1789) and Mr. Hill (Ellisland, March 2nd, 1790).

[50]Lord Rosebery, in an address delivered in Glasgow on the Centenary of the poet's death, July 21st, 1896, repr. in *The Complete Poetical Works of Robert Burns (Edinburgh, no date), p. xxxi*.

[51]*Loc. cit.*, pp. xxxix-xl.

Select Bibliography

The pioneer work of James Currie (1800) remains convenient and useful, while studies by modern scholars provide full and accurate accounts of various aspects of Burns's life and art. The standard edition of the poems and songs is that of James Kinsley (3 vols., 1968, 1 vol, 1969). The standard edition of the letters is that of John De Lancey Ferguson (2 vols., 1931), with a new one expected from G. Ross Roy. There are fine biographies by Franklyn Snyder (1932), Hans Hecht (1950), David Daiches (1971) and Robert Fitzhugh (1971), and fine critical studies include those of Auguste Angellier (1893), David Daiches (1950), Thomas Crawford (1960) and the collections of Donald Low (1974 and 1975).

Burns's Life and Works

Angellier,Auguste.Robert Burns. La Vie. Les Oeuvres. 2 vols. Paris, 1893.

Barke, James and Sydney G. Smith, eds. *The Merry Muses of Caledonia.* London, 1965.

Burns, Robert. *Poems, Chiefly in the Scottish Dialect.* Kilmarnock, 1786 (the 'Kilmarnock' edition), Edinburgh, 1787 (the 'Edinburgh' edition), Edinburgh, 1794 (the 'Second Edinburgh' edition).

Brown, Hilton. *There Was A Lad: An Essay on Robert Burns.* London, 1949.

Carswell, Catherine. *The Life of Robert Burns.* 2nd ed. London, 1951.

Chambers, Robert, ed. *The Life and Works of Robert Burns.* 4 vols. Edinburgh, 1851-2; rev. William Wallace, 4 vols., Edinburgh, 1896.

Crawford, Thomas. *Burns: A Study of the Poems and Songs.* Edinburgh, 1960, 1978.

_____ *Society and the Lyric: A Study of the Song Culture of Eighteenth Century Scotland.* Edinburgh, 1980.

Cromek, Robert Hartley, ed. *Reliques of Robert Burns.* London, 1808.

Cunningham, Allan, ed. *The Works of Robert Burns, with His Life.* 8 vols. London, 1834.

Currie, James, ed. *The Works of Robert Burns.* 4 vols. Liverpool, 1800; 5th ed., 4 vols., London, 1806.

_____, ed. *The Life and Works of Robert Burns, as Originally Edited by James Currie,* ed. Alexander Peterkin. 4 vols. Edinburgh, 1815.

_____, ed. *The Life of Robert Burns,* ed. James Currie and rev. Robert Chambers. Edinburgh, 1838.

Daiches, David. *Robert Burns.* London, 1952, 1970.

_____ *Robert Burns and his World.* London, 1971.

_____ *The Paradox of Scottish Culture.* London, 1964.

_____, ed. *The Selected Poems of Robert Burns*. Bungay, Suffolk, 1980.

Dick, James C., ed. *The Songs of Robert Burns*. London, 1903.

Douglas, Hugh. *Robert Burns — A Life*. Newton Abbot, 1977.

Douglas, William Scott, ed. *The Works of Robert Burns*. 6 vols. Edinburgh, 1877-9.

Ewing, J.C. and Davidson Cook, eds. *Robert Burns's Commonplace Book, 1783-1785*. Facsimile ed., Glasgow, 1938, repr. with introd. by David Daiches, 1965.

Ferguson, John Delancey. *Pride and Passion: Robert Burns 1759-1796*. New York, 1939.

_____, ed. *The Letters of Robert Burns*. 2 vols. Oxford, 1931.

Fitzhugh, Robert T. *Robert Burns: His Associates and Contemporaries*. Chapel Hill, N.C., 1943.

_____ *Robert Burns: The Man and the Poet*. Boston, 1970.

Gibson, James. *The Burns Calendar*. Kilmarnock, 1874, repr. New York, 1975.

Gray, Alexander. *Robert Burns — Man and Poet* *Edinburgh, 1944*.

Hecht, Hans. *Robert Burns: The Man and His Work*, trans. Jane Lymburn. 2nd ed., London, 1950.

Henley, W.E. and T.F. Henderson, eds. *The Poetry of Robert Burns*. 4 vols. Edinburgh, 1896-7 (the 'Centenary' edition).

Hogg, James and William Motherwell, eds. *The Works of Robert Burns*. 5 vols. Glasgow, 1838-41.

Johnson, James, ed. *The Scots Musical Museum*. 6 vols. Edinburgh, 1787-1803.

Kinsley, James, ed. *The Poems and Songs of Robert Burns*. 3 vols. Oxford, 1968. (1 vol., Oxford, 1969).

_____ *Scottish Poetry: A Critical Study*. London, 1955.

Legman, G., ed. *The Merry Muses of Caledonia*. New York, 1965.

Lindsey, Maurice. *Robert Burns: The Man; His Work; The Legend*. London, 1954; 4th ed., 1980.

_____ *The Burns Encyclopedia*. London, 1959; 2nd rev. ed., London, 1970.

Lockhart, John Gibson. *The Life of Robert Burns*. 2 vols. Liverpool, 1914.

Low, Donald A., ed. *Robert Burns: The Critical Heritage*. London, 1974.

_____ *Critical Essays on Robert Burns*. London, 1975.

_____ *Robert Burns: The Kilmarnock Poems*. London, 1985.

MacDiarmid, Hugh. *Burns Today and Tomorrow*. Edinburgh, 1959.

Montgomerie, William, ed. *New Judgments: Robert Burns*. Glasgow, 1947.

Pearl, Cyril. *Bawdy Burns*. London, 1958.

Renwick, W.L., ed. *Burns As Others Saw Him*. Edinburgh, 1959.

Robertson, J. Logie, ed. *The Poetical Works of Robert Burns*. Oxford, 1904, 1958.

Skinner, Basil C. *Robert Burns: Authentic Likenesses*. Edinburgh, 1963.
Smith, Syndney Goodsir, ed. *A Choice of Burns's Poems and Songs*. London, 1966.
Snyder, Franklin Bliss. *The Life of Robert Burns*. New York, 1932.
_____ *Robert Burns: His Personality, His Reputation & His Art*. Toronto, 1936.
Thomson, George, ed. *A Select Collection of Original Scottish Airs*. London, 1793-1818.
Thornton, Robert D. *James Currie: The Entire Stranger and Robert Burns*. Edinburgh, 1963.
_____, ed. *Robert Burns: Selected Poetry and Prose*. Boston, 1966.
_____ *William Maxwell to Robert Burns*. Edinburgh, 1980.
Wittig, Kurt. *The Scottish Tradition in Literature*. Edinburgh, 1958.
The Poetical Works of Robert Burns. The 'Albion' edition. London and New York, no date.

Language

Aitken, A.J. and Tom McArthur, eds. *Languages of Scotland*. Edinburgh, 1979.
Murison, David. *The Guid Scots Tongue*. Edinburgh, 1977, 1980.
_____ 'The Language of Burns', in Donald A Low, ed., *Critical Essays on Robert Burns*. London, 1975, pp. 54-69.
Reid, James B. *A Complete Word and Phrase Concordance to the Poems and Songs of Robert Burns*. Glasgow, 1889.
Wilson, Sir James. *The Dialect of Robert Burns as spoken in Central Ayrshire*. Oxford, 1923.
_____ *Scottish Poems of Robert Burns in his Native Dialect*. Oxford, 1925.
Scots Words From Burns: A Glossary of Words used in the Works of Robert Burns. Edinburgh, 1975.

Burns Country

Brown, R.L. *Robert Burns's Tour of the Borders*. Ipswich, 1972.
_____ *Robert Burns's Tours of the Highlands and Stirlingshire*. Ipswich, 1973.
Douglas, Hugh. *Portrait of the Burns Country*. London, 1968.
Fergus, Andrew. *Burns's Scotland*. Edinburgh, 1978.
Graham, Henry Grey. *The Social Life of Scotland in the Eighteenth Century*. London, 1901.
Guthrie, James A. *A Corner of Carrick*. Newton Stewart, 1979.

Henderson, T.F. *The Auld Ayrshire of Robert Burns*. London, 1906.
Letham, E.H. *Burns and Tarbolton*. Kilmarnock, 1900.
McDowall, William. *Robert Burns in Dumfriesshire*. Edinburgh, 1870.
McVie, John. *Robert Burns and Edinburgh*. Kilmarnock, 1969.
Prentice, Robin, ed. *The National Trust for Scotland Guide*. 2nd ed. London, 1978.
Shaw, James Edward. *Ayrshire 1745-1950*. Edinburgh, 1953.
Ayrshire at the Time of Burns. Ayrshire Archaeological and Natural History Society. Kilmarnock, 1959.

Collections of Scottish Jokes

Burnett, W.B., ed. *Scotland Laughing*. Edinburgh, 1955, 1956.
Elliot, A. & B., eds. *Best Scottish Jokes*. London, 1968, 1970.
Macgregor, Forbes, ed. *Doric Spice*. Edinburgh, 1956, 1960.
_____ *Macgregor's Mixture*. Edinburgh, 1976, 1981.
Nancy McPhee, ed. *The Book of Insults Ancient and Modern*. Toronto, 1978.

Select Discography

The Robert Burns Story. John Cairney. Radio Edinburgh Ltd. REL 448 (2 records).
A Night with Robert Burns. Jack Whyte, in association with the Calgary Burns Club. Westmount WSTM 7729.
The Songs of Robert Burns. Kenneth McKellar, with accompaniments directed by Bob Sharples. Decca PS 179.
Kenneth McKellar Sings Robert Burns. Kenneth McKellar, with orchestral arrangements by Peter Knight and Robert Sharples. Decca DPA 3045/6 (2 records).
The Robert Burns Songbook. Helen McArthur, Peter Morrison, Bill McCue, David Selley. Fiesta FLPS 1849.
Songs of Robert Burns. William McCue, accompanied by Patricia McCue. Scottish Records SRCM 139.
Tam o' Shanter and Songs by Robert Burns. Bill McCue, Bearsden Burgh Choir, conducted by Renton Thomson. The choral version of 'Tam o' Shanter' is by George MacIlwham, who also plays the pipes on the record. Lismor RB LP 1790.
The Poetry of Robert Burns. Frederick Worlock. Caedmon TC 1103.
The Love Songs of Robert Burns. Ann Moray. Spoken Arts 754.
Robert Burns in Poetry, Song and Prose. Arnold Johnston. CMS 614.

A Burns Country Itinerary

Welcome to the Land O' Burns!

Although Robert Burns spent several years of his life in Edinburgh, toured widely in both Highland and Lowland Scotland and, as exciseman, came to know the Solway Firth area very well, there is no doubt that 'the Burns Country' for the tourist means really those areas of Ayrshire and Dumfriesshire frequented by the national bard. It is certainly on the south-western corner of Scotland that tourist activity for lovers of the poet is centred, and it is in this part of the country that memorials and memorabilia abound. Indeed, it has frequently been remarked that if all the contents of all the Burns museums were gathered in one spot, we should find that our impoverished ploughman in fact owned a large number of assorted possessions, and the biographies might well have to place less emphasis on the poet's poverty.

Access to the Burns Country is very easy. For the visitor from abroad, Prestwick International Airport provides immediate entry, with Alloway only 5 miles away. From England, take the M6 from Birmingham (bypassing Carlisle), then the A74 to Gretna and the A75 to Dumfries; from Dumfries, the A76 runs directly to Kilmarnock. The Scot has only 25 miles to come southwards from Glasgow on the A77. For general information, contact:

The Scottish Tourist Board,
23 Ravelston Terrace,
Edinburgh.   EH4 3EU   Tel. (031)332.2433

The obvious centre in which to stay is Ayr, which gives ready access to most of the usual places of Burns interest except for Dumfries. The more adventurous seek accommodation in the charming little villages of Kyle and Carrick, and are never disappointed. The best place at which to start one's tour is not in Ayr, however, but a couple of miles to the south, in Alloway, at the splendid Land o' Burns Centre, opposite the Auld Haunted Kirk and five minutes' walk from the Brig o' Doon.

Developed by the Kyle and Carrick District Council with the assistance of the Scottish Tourist Board, the Land o' Burns Centre handles about 140,000 visitors per year. Inside the building, facilities include an information centre, an Audio-Visual Theatre with a multi-screen projection of a fine programme of slides, readings and songs, and a souvenir shop selling a wide range of goods — Scottish jewellery, glass, pottery, leather goods, woollen goods, books, maps, posters, postcards and records. Outside, the building is surrounded by beautifully landscaped gardens, picnic areas, and car and coach parks. The Centre is managed by the Parks and Recreation Department of the Kyle and Carrick District Council, and is open daily, including Sundays, from 10-6. For further information, contact:

The Manager,
Land o' Burns Centre,
Alloway, Ayr.   Tel. (0292)43700

Be sure to ask also for details of the annual Burns Festival, a week of celebration including music, poetry, exhibitions, symposia, folk-concerts, a Holy Fair and Burns Days. The dates usually fall in early June, the latest Festivals being held on June 8th-16th, 1985 and June 7th-15th, 1986.

Do not concentrate on Burns to the exclusion of all else, otherwise you will miss some very attractive scenery, some lovely little villages like Kirkmichael or Straiton, some impressive ruins like those of Crossraguel Abbey, a former Cluniac establishment (1244-1592) near Maybole, and some remarkable castles. Among the latter, be sure to visit the former home of the Maxwell family, Caerlaverock Castle, a moated castle dating back to 1220 and renovated (with some fine carving) in the seventeenth century, and Culzean Castle, former home of the Earls of Cassillis (later Marquesses of Ailsa) and one of Robert Adam's architectural masterpieces. For further information, contact:

The South West Scotland
(Dumfries and Galloway) Tourist Association,
Douglas House,
Newton Stewart,
Wigtownshire.   Tel. (0671)2549

Mention of Culzean Castle, given by the 5th Marquess of Ailsa to the National Trust, serves to focus attention on one of the tourist world's finest bargains — membership of the National Trust for Scotland. The very modest annual membership fee for an individual or a family virtually pays for itself in the money saved on the first day's entrance and parking charges. Membership of the Scottish Trust carries with it reciprocal membership of the corresponding English body, but is the cheaper of the two! The address to contact is:

The National Trust for Scotland,
5 Charlotte Square,
Edinburgh.   EH2 4DU   Tel. (031)226.5922

Alloway

Alloway is the obvious starting-point for a Burns Tour just as it is the obvious site for the Land o' Burns Centre, for it was in Alloway that Robert Burns was born on January 25th, 1759, the eldest of seven children born to William Burness (a cottar from Kincardineshire) and Agnes Brown from nearby Kirkoswald. The parents met at a fair in Maybole in 1756 and married in 1757. William Burness acquired 7 1/2 acres of land at Alloway, 6 acres of which still belong to the Burns Monument Trustees, and built thereon the 'auld clay biggin'. The whitewashed clay cottage was sold in 1781 for £160 to the Incorporation of Shoemakers in Ayr and spent much of the next hundred years as a public house until it was purchased in 1881 for £4,000 by the Alloway Burns Monument Trustees and lovingly

Kirk Alloway

restored. The poet spent his earliest years in Alloway, attending school at the age of 6 at Alloway Mill beside the River Doon.

The birth cottage and the associated museum are virtually a stone's throw from the Auld Haunted Kirk which was to be of literary significance towards the end of the poet's life. Kirk Alloway was last used in 1756, so it was already a roofless ruin when Burns was a youngster. The poet's father William Burness (1721-84) is buried in the churchyard, although Agnes Brown is buried far away, in Ballan churchyard in East Lothian. Kirk Alloway is, of course, most important as the setting for the witches' black mass in *Tam o' Shanter*

> When, glimmering thro' the groaning trees,
> Kirk-Alloway seem'd in a bleeze;
> Thro' ilka bore the beams were glancing;
> And loud resounded mirth and dancing.

Across the road, in a pleasant park overlooking the River Doon, is rather a strange monument, one erected ostensibly in memory of a Romantic poet but built in the Classical style. The Burns Monument was conceived in 1814 and completed in 1823. Items on display include

The Auld Brig O' Doon

a bust of Burns by Patric Park and duplicates of the Thom figures in Kirkoswald which commemorate Tam o' Shanter and Soutar Johnnie.

The 13th-century Brig o' Doon still spans the river just as it did in Burns's childhood and will do for ever at the climax of *Tam o' Shanter* when Nannie almost catches the world's most famous tippler:

> Ae spring brought off her master hale,
> But left behind her ain gray tail:
> The carlin claught her by the rump,
> And left poor Maggie scarce a stump.

One and a half miles south-east of Alloway is Mount Oliphant Farm at Doonholm, whither the Burness family moved when Robert was 7 and where they all experienced nothing but poverty and straitened circumstances for the eleven years from 1766-1777.

Kirkoswald

This pleasant little village was supposedly founded by St. Oswald in 634, in gratitude for the winning of a great but now long-forgotten battle. The bard's mother, Agnes Brown, was a native of Kirkoswald, and in 1775 Burns came here while in his teens to live with an uncle, to attend the school of Hugh Roger, and to meet 'scenes of swaggering riot and roaring dissipation'. Burns came to Hugh Roger's school to learn land-surveying and mathematics, but stayed to learn of matters which were to prove very much more significant in his later life:

> A charming Fillette who lived next door to the school overset my Trigonomertry, and set me off in a tangent from the sphere of my studies . . . stepping out to the garden one charming noon, to take the sun's altitude, I met with my Angel . . . the two last nights of my stay in the country, had sleep been a mortal sin, I was innocent . . . I returned home very considerably improved.

Kirkoswald joins Alloway in being famous because of the poem *Tam o' Shanter*. In the graveyard, clearly marked for tourists, are the last resting-places of Hugh Roger, the teacher; relatives of Agnes Brown; Jean Kennedy (Kirkton Jean); Douglas Graham (Tam o' Shanter); and John Davidson (Soutar Johnnie). Opposite the grave-yard is still preserved Soutar Johnnie's House, though the original Kirkton Jean's hostelry is no more. The Rev. James Muir, minister of Kirkoswald 1890-1931, is responsible for preserving the graves and the cottage, which is now a National Trust property.

John Davidson's house, built in 1785, is nicely restored, fur-nished with period fittings and equipped with antique soutar's tools. In the wee garden out the back are four stone figures representing Tam o' Shanter, Soutar Johnnie, the landlord and his wife (a Mr. and Mrs. Shearer):

> The landlady and Tam grew gracious,
> Wi' favours, secret, sweet, and precious:
> The Souter tauld his queerest stories;
> The landlord's laugh was ready chorus:
> The storm without might rair and rustle,
> Tam did na mind the storm a whistle.

The figures, 1 1/2 times life size, were sculpted by James Thom, a native of Tarbolton, in 1828. While awaiting transfer to their pre-sent location, the figures stood temporarily in the minister's garden and, weighing around a ton apiece, rapidly began to sink out of sight into the minister's lawn. They are now built upon surer foundations!

Soutar Johnnie and His House, Kirkoswald

Ayr

The seaside market town dating back to the thirteenth century is a bustling tourist centre with a pleasant beach and two nice parks, Belleisle and Craigie. Ayr figures in *Tam o' Shanter* as the starting-point of Tam's ride:

> Auld Ayr, wham ne'er a town surpasses,
> For honest men and bonny lasses.

In the High Street, the Tam o' Shanter Inn, supposedly the ale-house to which Douglas Graham of Shanter Farm delivered his malted grain, is now a Burns Museum.

Burns was baptized in the 17th-century Auld Kirk (built 1654-1656) and for three weeks studied in Ayr in 1773 with John Murdoch, who taught first in the little school in Alloway. The 13th-century foot-bridge which figures in Burns's poem *The Brigs of Ayr* is asked by the New Brig:

> Will your poor, narrow foot-path of a street,
> Where twa wheel-barrows tremble when they meet,
> Your ruin'd, formless bulk o' stane and lime,
> Compare wi' bonie Brigs o' modern time?

Tam O' Shanter Museum, Ayr

The Auld Brig survives, but as it prophesied in the poem its newer rival was reduced to 'a shapeless cairn' by a storm and has been replaced.

In Burns Statue Square stands a statue of Burns, facing south to his birthplace at Alloway, about 2 miles away. A duplicate of the statue looks from Stanley Park over the boats and sky-scrapers of far-away Vancouver.

Tarbolton

As its etymology suggests, the name 'Tarbolton' signifies a former centre of Baal-worship, and a public bonfire in the village every June commemorates the old pagan festival of Bealltainn. The Burness family came here in 1777 when Robert was 18, and worked the farm of Lochlea very inefficiently until the death of William Burness in 1784. One gets the impression that the Burness family were never the most skilful of farmers, for Lochlea Farm is cultivated today with great success.

The Bachelors' Club, Tarbolton

Lochlea Farm can be seen across the fields from a small, white-washed, thatched 17th-century cottage in Tarbolton which figured large in the experience of the young poet. In 1779 Robert took dancing lessons in the house, then in 1780 founded the Bachelors' Club with his brother Gilbert and the other young men of the district. In 1781, in the same house, the poet was installed as a freemason in Lodge St. David. (Later, 1784-88, he became Depute Master of Lodge St. James, Tarbolton.)

The Bachelors' Club met every fourth Monday to debate and drink toasts under a series of elaborate rules. The poet is usually held to have been responsible for this final rule:

> 10th. Every man proper for a member of this society, must have a frank, honest, open heart; above anything dirty or mean; and must be a professed lover of one or more of the female sex. No haughty, self-conceited person, who looks upon himself as superior to the rest of the club, and especially no mean-spirited, worldly mortal, whose only will is to heap up money, shall upon any pretence whatever be admitted. In short, the proper person for this society is, a cheerful, honest-hearted lad, who, if he has a friend that is true, and a mistress that is kind, and as much wealth as genteely to make both ends meet — is just as happy as this world can make him.

Since 1971 an annual Burns Supper has been held in the Bachelors' Club, the only modern venue essentially unchanged since the poet's time. The cottage is now a property of the National Trust for Scotland, and the caretaker, Sam Hay, will be delighted to show you round.

Mauchline

Following the death of William Burness in 1784, Robert moved the family to Mossgiel Farm at the north end of the town of Mauchline. Again, hard times were the reward of the family's labours, Robert and Gilbert allowing themselves only a workman's annual wage of £7. (The farm, rebuilt, is now in private hands.)

Mauchline is important to the poet's biography because of the poet's affair with and later marriage to Jean Armour, daughter of a local mason. Burns did not take long to get Jean pregnant, with twins born in 1786 but not long-lived. The appearance of the Kilmarnock

Burns's House, Mauchline

edition led the poet to abandon plans to emigrate to Jamaica and brought him back to Mauchline and Jean.

Next to Mauchline Castle can still be seen the home of Gavin Hamilton in which the poet married Jean before taking her to his own house in Castle Street in February of 1788. Later that year Jean bore a further set of twins, also very short-lived. Burns and his wife lived in the house in Castle Street until their move to Ellisland Farm, north of Dumfries. The Mauchline house is now a museum, the curator living next door in what used to be the home of John Mackenzie, the poet's physician and friend. The other Mauchline memorial to the poet is the National Burns Memorial Tower, standing above the Cottage Homes founded in 1896.

While resident in Mauchline Burns produced not only *The Cotter's Saturday Night* but also his attacks on the Auld Licht Calvinist Church found in such poems as *Holy Willie's Prayer* and *The Holy Fair*. Mauchline churchyard, the scene of *The Holy Fair*, contains several notable graves — those of Burns's four tiny children, Rev. William (Daddy) Auld, Robert Wilson, Gavin Hamilton, James Humphrey (the 'bleth'ran bitch') and William Fischer (Holy Willie):

> I bless and praise thy matchless might,
> When thousands thou has left in night,
> That I am here before thy sight,
>   For gifts and grace,
> A burning and a shining light
>   To a' this place.

Opposite the kirkyard is the tavern of Poosie Nansie, in real life Agnes Gibson who with her husband George kept the ale-house and lodging-house (still in use) in which Burns found the sitters for the portraits of low characters he painted in *The Jolly Beggars: A Cantata.* Modern-day Mauchline must be a quieter place than it was in Burns's time!

Failford

In 1786, the knowledge Burns had acquired at school in Kirkoswald started to show results. The poet had already had an illegitimate child by Elizabeth Paton when he got Jean Armour in the family way, too, and embarked upon a common-law relationship with her. Jean's father not unnaturally objecting to the 'marriage', Burns next transferred his affections to Highland Mary, intending to emigrate to Jamaica and to take Mary with him as his wife.

Highland Mary, Mary Campbell of Auchnamore, near Dunoon, accepted the poet's proposal of marriage, but her death shortly after brought their love to an end. It was in Failford, at a spot now marked by a monument, that Burns and his Mary had their last meeting, exchanging Bibles and plighting their troth on Sunday, May 14th. By the autumn, Mary was gone:

> That sacred hour can I forget,
>   Can I forget the hallowed grove,
> Where by the winding Ayr we met,
>   To live one day of Parting Love?
> Eternity can not efface
>   Those records dear of transports past;
> Thy image at our last embrace,
>   Ah, little thought we 'twas our last!

Highland Mary lies buried at Greenock, and there is a statue at Dunoon in memory of her brief life (1763-86).

Failford

Kilmarnock

Truth to tell, I personally do not find Kilmarnock the most exciting of the halts on the Burns Heritage Trail. True, there are Burns links here — Dean Castle, the Laigh and Old High Kirks, the 100-year-old Burns Monument in Kay Park — but they tend to disappoint the pilgrim a little. Tam Samson's House, for instance, is grey and undistinguished, and there is no sign now of the printer's establishment which made the poet famous overnight on the eve of his departure for exile in Jamaica. On July 31st, 1786, John Wilson published the Kilmarnock edition of Burns's poems which made the poet's name and put £20 in his pocket. It is disappointing not to see his business, only the famed edition.

Ellisland

On the way to Dumfries to conclude the tracing of Burns's life, stop at Ellisland Farm, some 6 miles to the north of Dumfries, in Nithsdale and on the west bank of the River Nith. Robert Burns came here from Mauchline in 1788 and constructed the present farmhouse. He was obviously a better builder than a cottar, for again his attempts at farming proved distastrous and led to his becoming an Exciseman instead. Ellisland Farm is open to the public, and offers to view the restored granary and an agricultural museum.

Dumfries

Burn's Death-House, Dumfries

Dumfries is an attractive town, boasting the marvelous prospect of the splendid old, mediaeval bridge built over the River Nith by Devorguilla Balliol in the thirteenth century. For the Burns enthusiast, there is the prospect of a drink in Burns's 'favourite howff', the Globe Inn, followed by a visit to the Burns Statue, erected in April, 1882. Most important, however, are the death-house in Mill Vennel and the Mausoleum in the kirkyard of St. Michael's.

Burns the Exciseman came to Dumfries in November, 1791, taking up residence first in a miserable, three-room flat in the Wee Vennel (now Bank Street). In May, 1793, the poet moved to a better neighbourhood, to the red sandstone house in the Mill Vennel (now Burns Street) in which he was to die rather wretchedly just over three years later, on July 21st, 1796. His widow dwelt in the house until her own passing, at age 69, in 1834, and the house is now a museum. The plaque on the wall reads as follows:

In this house the Scottish National Poet Robert Burns died on 21st July 1796. After his decease his wife Jean Armour (Bonnie Jean) continued to reside here until her death in 1834. The mortal remains of the poet and his wife are interred in the kirkyard of St. Michael's situated nearby. In 1851 this house was purchased by the poet's son Colonel William Nicol Burns E.I.C.S. and placed by him under the care of trustees for its maintenance as far as possible in perpetuity as a memorial to his father.

The plaque does not, of course, tell the whole story of the poet's miserable death and unfortunate funeral. Burns was buried four days after his passing, on July 25th, 1796, but his wife was not in attendance, being occupied in giving birth to their last child, a boy ironically named Maxwell after the doctor whose treatments did much to hasten the poet's death. And poor Burns was accorded the very sort of funeral he had specifically refused — a military one during the course of which the Gentlemen Volunteers of Dumfries (the 'Awkward Squad') fired ragged volleys over the grave, as Burns had feared they might. The grave, moreover, was a very modest one almost lost in a hidden corner of the kirkyard.

When the poet was safely dead, of course, he could be accorded the honour denied him in life. On September 19th, 1815, the bard's remains were removed from the first grave and transferred to the opposite corner of the graveyard, into a splendid Mausoleum which is built, it seems to me, in a Classical style more appropriate to the gentle weather of the Mediterranean than to the rigours of a Scottish clime. Here, however, end most Burns pilgrimages, in the quiet of the old kirkyard, with the words of the spae-wife echoing in the inner ear:

> He'll hae misfortunes great and sma',
> But aye a heart aboon them a';
> He'll be a credit till us a',
>   We'll a' be proud o' Robin.

Fair fa' ye a' in the Land o' Burns!

The Mausoleum, Dumfries

The Mausoleum, Dumfries

Index A: *Burns's Works*

Index B: People and Places

Index C: Photographs